PINPOINT

PINPOINT

How challenging the norm is the only route
to success in selling sponsorship

JACKIE/FAST

LIONCREST
PUBLISHING

PINPOINT

*How challenging the norm is the only route
to success in selling sponsorship*

ISBN   978-1-61961-818-3 *Paperback*
         978-1-61961-819-0 *Ebook*

To everyone who wants to do things better.

And to Jay-Z, who keeps me hustlin'.

CONTENTS

FOREWORD 9

INTRODUCTION.................................... 13

1. THE OLD RULES NO LONGER APPLY.............. 29

2. DON'T MAKE IT ABOUT YOU 49

3. IT'S NOT ABOUT WHAT YOU NEED 71

4. LEARN THE FUNDAMENTALS..........................103

5. IT'S NOT WHO YOU KNOW 121

6. WHY PEOPLE AVOID SPONSORSHIP 137

CONCLUSION..153

AFTERWORD: THE STORY OF SLINGSHOT.....161

APPENDIX 173

CONTACT JACKIE 175

FOREWORD

The success story of how I launched and built a global sponsorship agency is the embodiment of one of my favourite maxims. It comes from Irish playwright Samuel Beckett. The modern version of the adage goes like this:

Try, fail, try again, fail a little less, try again, fail a little less, try again, succeed.

That's how my career in sponsorship began, by making every mistake in the book, as well as many that weren't even in the book, until I figured out a better way—a way that worked.

In those difficult years of struggle, I learned why some sponsorship pitches fail, and why others succeed. I figured out the six key elements that are essential to being successful in sponsorship sales. In this book, I'm sharing what I've learned over ten years in sponsorship, so you don't have to go through what I went through, and what thousands of our clients have gone through.

There are six key strategies, or lessons, that I want you to take away and then implement. You can't do just one or two of them; you have to understand and employ all six. If you do, the rewards will be worth it.

For reasons I will explain, I believe sponsorship is the future of business. Sponsorship is an essential element of any organisation's marketing mix. Embrace it and watch profits rise and engagement soar. Ignore it at your own peril.

Do not mistake this book for a "how to do sponsorship" guide. It isn't a how-to book at all. So, if you're expecting a step-by-step, one-size-fits-all, paint-by-numbers road map showing you how to do sponsorship, then perhaps other books on the topic will serve you better.

But, if you want to really understand the bedrock principles of sponsorship success, you've come to the right place. The content is unlike that of any other book you've read on sponsorship. I won't coddle you, the reader, because that's a waste of your time. And mind. I'll tell it to you straight. I won't pull punches. I won't worry about offending your delicate sponsorship sensibilities. If you're an experienced sponsorship professional, I will likely challenge your beliefs. You might even learn that you've been doing it wrong for all these years.

My goal is to inspire people at all levels—from veteran sponsorship teams to absolute beginners looking for their first-ever sponsor—to do sponsorship better. As they say, a rising tide lifts all boats. The more people who understand these six principles of sponsorship, the better off the entire industry will be.

I love sponsorship. It has given me so much. My greatest wish is to see it, and you, excel, expand, and prosper. It all starts with building a strong foundation. The six strategies you're about to learn will provide a solid base for many years of success in sponsorship.

INTRODUCTION

BIRTH OF A MEGA-INDUSTRY

Sweat dripped off the faces of the elite German athletes. Their jaws clenched. Muscles tightened. Hands trembled. Minds completely focused on the task ahead. You could see the intensity on their faces. They were preparing for one of the most important, nerve-wracking, and consequential moments in their careers—in all of sport, in fact.

What happened on this day in 1973 would change their lives forever. It would change football forever. There would be no turning back.

The team members of the German Bundesliga football team, Eintracht Braunschweig, were on the cusp of a truly monumental victory. Oddly, there were no fervent football fans cheering them on. They weren't in a stadium. The players weren't even wearing their uniforms.

This wasn't the final game in the German Super Cup championship. It wasn't a football match at all. It was a team meeting.

Why all the drama?

Because the outcome of this meeting would have epic consequences that would reverberate around the world. What happened in that meeting literally would transform football, professional and college sports, business, marketing, and branding, and it would create thousands of jobs and billions of dollars in revenue. The impact would be far beyond what anyone in that room could have imagined at the time.

The players on the Eintracht Braunschweig football team cast their votes. They had gathered to take an important vote. It was an unprecedented vote that would blatantly defy the wishes of the Bundesliga. By voting in favour of the proposed resolution, they were risking everything. But they knew it was the right thing to do.

The votes were quickly counted. The motion passed. The

Eintracht team had just voted to officially change the logo on the front of their team jerseys from their team emblem to a curious new logo featuring a stag and glowing cross.

It was the logo of German liqueur brand Jägermeister.

A few years earlier, Günter Mast, the nephew of Jägermeister creator Curt Mast, approached Eintracht and offered to pay the team if they would emblazon the Jägermeister logo on their game-day jerseys. The team said yes, but the Bundesliga said no. At that time, most sports leagues throughout Europe staunchly opposed the idea and prohibited teams from putting any logo on their jerseys, other than their official team logo.

It was the same story in the Bundesliga. League rules mandated that each member team had the right to display only their team's *official logo* on their uniforms. So, if the team held a vote and adopted the Jägermeister stag and cross as their official team logo, there was nothing the league could do to stop it.

With that one important vote by Eintracht Braunschweig, the floodgates opened. It ushered in a new era of sports sponsorship that would soon take root in every professional sport all over the world. Jägermeister paid Eintracht between 160,000 and 800,000 Deutschmarks over five years in what is widely accepted as the very first logo on a jersey professional sports sponsorship deal.

On March 23, 1973, the team debuted their new sponsor in the first official match wearing the new jerseys. The fans reacted positively. The Bundesliga was paying close attention. They immediately saw the potential for vast new revenue streams into the sport. Seven months later, the league officially sanctioned jersey sponsorship.

A mega-industry was born.

NOT MUCH HAS CHANGED

In the forty-five years since, a lot has changed—just not in sponsorship. The world has seen the invention of the smartphone, the space shuttle, electric cars, the internet, the iPod, Facebook, Instagram, Snapchat, Uber, and a million other incredible, life-altering inventions and innovations that changed the world as we knew it. Human ingenuity has transformed, disrupted, and elevated most of the industries on earth, from medical technology to space travel to farming and food production.

But not sponsorship.

Incredibly, the fundamental business of sponsorship has

remained relatively unchanged over the last half century. For the vast majority of agencies and organisations that participate in this field, the basic sponsorship model works the same way now as it did back in the days when the Eintracht players were wearing polyester pants and listening to music by the Scorpions and ABBA.

With so much disruption and advancement in almost every sector and industry, it's shocking that practices and principles used fifty years ago still exist today. I will argue that because of this lack of advancement, everyone is failing at sponsorship. But put simply, it's easy to fix. We just need to go against everything we thought we knew.

WHO SHOULD READ THIS BOOK

Everybody has something they want to do in the world that sponsorship could help with. That could be anything from selling rights to a global organisation to enlisting a local grocery store to support a community playground. If you've never considered that sponsorship could work for you, I want you to realise that it could, regardless of the size of your organisation.

By the same token, don't assume that sponsorship isn't for you just because you don't have worldwide brand recognition, a huge agency at your back, or an address book full of contacts. Those things can be helpful, of course, but they're not necessary.

Whether you oversee a billion-pound corporation, a global charity, or a national arts council, or you coach a children's football team, manage a community theatre, own a small chain of dry cleaners, or are launching a start-up, this book is for you. Regardless of the size and financial resources of your organisation, sponsorship is something that can benefit you immensely.

This book is designed to help any person or organisation be successful in sponsorship. The sponsorship industry is finally beginning to think beyond the tired old model of slapping a logo on a sports jersey, and that is creating tremendous opportunity for organisations of all shapes and sizes.

By the end of this book, you'll have a clear picture of the tremendous opportunities available for brands and rights holders who understand the present and future of sponsorship. Many of the greatest opportunities in sponsorship today have sprouted out of the challenges and traditions of the past. My goal is to give you a results-driven perspective to appreciate the true potential that partnerships can bring to business growth.

Whether you're a sponsorship veteran, are new to sponsorship, or are thinking about adding sponsorship into your marketing mix for the first time, the content in these pages will help you immensely. If you work for an organisation seeking to *sell* sponsorship, or a brand that *buys* sponsorship, this book will help you succeed. If you want to create significant revenue and drive further brand value from activity you already invest in, these principles will help.

BE PREPARED FOR NEW IDEAS

Be prepared. The ideas here will challenge you. This book will question the accepted practices employed for decades by professionals and executives in the sponsorship industry. If you're not open to learning the six keys to successfully selling sponsorship, many of which are counterintuitive and go against long-held beliefs in this industry, then perhaps a different book would serve you better. However, if you are willing to think differently about what's always been done in sponsorship, and you're ready to try a new approach, this book is for you.

There are plenty of books published on the topic of sponsorship. It is a $60 billion industry, after all. But most of those sponsorship books focus on a generic process and how-to steps. Unfortunately, that won't help you. Each sponsorship situation and relationship is different from the next, so a series of general steps won't serve you well. Plus, if you've worked in the industry for more than six months, you already know the process and the steps. Even if you're brand new to sponsorship, you'll quickly learn the ropes anyway, so you don't need a book to tell you, "First do this; next do this." Anyone can learn a process.

There are zero books like this one.

This book will give you information and a perspective that is infinitely more valuable than a process and steps. To do sponsorship well, you need a new way of thinking. In the coming chapters, you'll learn a new framework of thinking about sponsorship that will allow you to succeed.

Too many organisations spin their wheels doing things they *think* they should be doing to get sponsors, but their strategy is wrong, and they end up wasting time and resources. It's time to stop doing what doesn't work and focus on what does.

MARKETING AND ADVERTISING HAS CHANGED

The world of marketing, branding, and advertising has changed dramatically in the past decade. New forms of communication using smartphones, mobile apps, cloud computing, and social media have disrupted the way consumers engage with brands. The traditional marketing methods that brands have used for decades to influence consumer buying decisions simply don't work anymore. Television commercials, magazine ads, billboards, and traditional advertising campaigns have lost their effectiveness.

Similarly, the sponsorship industry is now facing external market pressures that are going to force the industry to change, whether it wants to or not. Brands paying big money for logo placement was once a standard practice, because it worked. But in the Information Age, those days are rapidly coming to an end. The entire sponsorship industry is entering a period of massive upheaval, and new rules apply.

Sponsorship is now much more complex. Today, sponsors evaluate return on investment (ROI) not just through financial return, but also through social shares, traffic, engagement, and a range of other metrics that didn't exist twenty years ago. Some of the largest social platforms today didn't exist even ten years ago. As of this writing, Snapchat is six years old. Instagram is barely seven.

If you work in sponsorship, you need to understand this new paradigm and learn to adapt. If you've never considered sponsorship as a marketing tool or as a revenue source for your organisation, this is the best time in history to start.

SPONSORSHIP IS MY LIFE

I get fired up about this stuff because it has been my life's passion for my entire professional career. I eat and sleep sponsorship. I mean that literally; I relentlessly eat lunch at my desk and work through the day building sponsorship proposals, and I truly dream about creating great sponsorships. Sad, I know.

But the payoff is worth it. When great sponsorships come together and the brand, the rights holder, and the audience are all thrilled with the result it's exhilarating. It's fun. Everyone is happy, satisfied, and looking for the next opportunity to do it again.

Unfortunately, that's not the typical experience in this industry.

When sponsorship doesn't work, it can be a disaster. Let's forget for a moment the thousands or millions of pounds wasted on a partnership that flopped and didn't achieve the desired objective. From a customer, human capital, and relationship perspective, a bad sponsorship can be devastating. At the very least, no one wants to work together again. At the worst, reputations and careers can be damaged or destroyed. Don't let that happen to you.

A NEW PARADIGM IN SPONSORSHIP

My team and I do things differently. We pioneered a new paradigm in sponsorship. Ten years ago, what we did was unheard of; but today it's starting to catch on as people witness the power of our framework and the results we achieve for our partners.

We have experience successfully selling sponsorships and partnerships in the current market for hundreds of client organisations of all sizes. I have seen too many organisations fail at sponsorship, and I understand why they fail. They make the same mistakes that everyone else is making. So, I devised a better way and launched a company to help organisations capitalize on it.

That way provides a maximum benefit for everyone—sponsors, rights holders, and customers. Teaching those strategies is the purpose of this book. I chose the book's title, *Pinpoint*, to highlight the importance of being strategic and narrowing the focus to a specific, targeted result.

The way we do sponsorship was developed by spending nearly a decade in the trenches, and it creates the greatest likelihood of success; but it's not the easiest or quickest way. It takes more time and effort. We embrace a long-term view, and we focus on building lasting value and benefit for all of our partners. We're not interested in making a fast buck by flogging sports-kit branding.

That's not what we do. We are strategic thinkers. We like a challenge. We want our work to mean something and deliver exceptional results.

Right about now you're probably thinking, "Who is writing this, anyway? Who is this Jackie Fast lady? What makes her qualified to write a book on sponsorship?" Fair questions. I'm happy to answer them. I will tell you my whole story starting from the beginning. I'll explain how I got into sponsorship, the obstacles I overcame, and how I built one of the most respected sponsorship sales agencies in the world.

But because I'm a bit of a *Chatty Cathy*, and because I respect your time, I'll get straight to the meat of this book first—the six key sponsorship principles. Then I'll tell my story at the end. If you're still reading at that point, then I think you'll enjoy my story and learn some lessons from it.

Right now, let's get to the important stuff.

A BRIEF SKETCH OF THE INDUSTRY

Sponsorship is a powerful force. Used well, sponsorship can be a highly effective way of leveraging connections to create mutually beneficial partnerships. Unfortunately, most people don't look beyond the surface to explore the true long-term potential of a sponsorship. They think that sponsorship means putting a logo on a shirt, a programme, or a stage. It can be and needs to be so much more than that.

The old logo-on-a-shirt approach used to work well. Nike literally built a multibillion-dollar shoe and apparel empire by paying teams and athletes to put their Swoosh on sports jerseys. For years, that was enough. It isn't enough any longer. In fact, I would argue that slapping a logo on a shirt isn't sponsorship at all; it's moving advertising.

Brands are spending fortunes on sponsorship, and the need to understand and measure ROI and value from marketing or sponsorship activity is critical. Rights holders still do not fully understand this.

Most rights holders look at sponsorship from the wrong perspective. They need money, and they see sponsorship as an opportunity to get that money. What they forget is something that everyone learns as a child, but most of us ignore when we become adults. Two heads are better than one, and a symbiotic collaboration enriches everyone. When sponsorship is done right, it pools energy, resources, people, and insights; and the results are far greater than either party could have achieved on their own. That's the true power of sponsorship. It's not just about putting your logo on a stadium door.

Done well, sponsorship brings you things you can't buy, enabling you to do things you couldn't do before. It's not just about money. It's about achieving greater results through leveraging the strengths and talents that each organisation brings to the partnership. Does putting a logo on a shirt fulfil that goal? I believe that nine times out of ten, it doesn't.

Brands want to approach sponsorship more effectively, but most are too set in their ways to experiment with a new approach. Agencies know they could create more value for their clients, but, so far, the market doesn't encourage them to do so. They are financially incentivised to promote a limited model of sponsorship. They go after the low-hanging fruit. Thinking more innovatively would cut into their bottom line because it takes more time and effort.

HOW TO USE THIS BOOK

This book is not designed to be a toolkit, because a toolkit won't address your individual needs. In this business, one size does *not* fit all, and every client and project is unique. The book will, however, give you a perspective on sponsorship that you may never have heard before, and it will encourage you to do your own creative thinking about how that could translate to your business. The goal is to spark your imagination, not kill it with a prescriptive approach.

In the following six chapters I will tackle some of the most common misconceptions about what sponsorship is and how to do it well. Hopefully, it will take some of the smoke and mirrors out of the industry, and give you a chance to think for yourself about how best to utilise a partnership approach in business. Regardless of the size and scope of your business, sponsorship can help achieve your goals.

There is far more to sponsorship than you may think, but you must approach it with creativity and an open mind. I came into the industry as an outsider, and I remain sceptical about many mainstream sponsorship industry practices. I am now more convinced than ever that there is a way to do sponsorship better, a way that delivers genuine value to everyone involved.

The flip side of this belief, however, is that doing sponsorship well requires work and emotional investment. You won't find a simple step-by-step guide to sponsorship here, because there *is* no simple step-by-step route to getting it right. Any book or expert who claims otherwise is misleading. When you find your own path, perhaps inspired by the stories and guided by the principles you'll discover in the coming chapters, I hope you'll realise it can be a very inspiring and profitable way of doing business.

CHAPTER ONE

THE OLD RULES NO LONGER APPLY

I used to dream about travel. I always viewed airports as places where adventure began. When I was a teenager in Canada, I wanted to be a flight attendant for one of the airlines. I liked the concept of jetting off to foreign cities, meeting interesting passengers, getting paid to travel, and looking for love, or at least romance. It all sounded so exotic and exciting.

Alas, I was in Canada and the airlines required all flight attendants to speak fluent French. I didn't. So, my dreams of a passport adorned with colourful stamps would have to wait.

Fast-forward twenty years, and that dream came true for

me—sort of. Well, not the becoming a flight attendant part, and perhaps not the exotic and exciting part, but at least the travel part. Business travel, that is. Today, I'm on an international flight about once a week.

Business travel takes a lot of time, planning, work, and energy. It's draining. Nevertheless, the smell of jet fuel mixed with diesel fumes and the joy of watching eight hours of uninterrupted new releases still excites me. Unfortunately, when I fly all day, by the time I get to the hotel, I'm too exhausted to go out and explore a new city. I want to collapse in a heap on the bed, but always with a comfy pillow.

I now understand the value of a high-quality pillow. Over thousands of nights in hundreds of hotels, I've learned that pillows are where otherwise expensive luxury hotels skimp to save money. That bothers me because fine pillows are necessary to enjoying my stay in a hotel—pillows, *and* ideally a few Picante de la Casa cocktails.

PILLOWS IN HONG KONG

The British Airways 747 was packed, a full flight from Heathrow to Hong Kong. It's always amazed me how such a heavy object, weighed down with luggage, fuel, passengers, and God knows what slithering around in the cargo hold, could even get off the ground, let alone fly nine thousand kilometres nonstop. We'd be passing over the Netherlands, Belgium, Germany, Poland, Belarus, Russia, Kazakhstan, Mongolia, China, and perhaps a country or two I didn't know existed. It is such a long way in distance. But to me, it was twelve hours of sitting uncomfortably, drifting in and out of shallow sleep, and arriving with dry eyes, messy hair, and a sore neck.

That flight was many years ago when I took my first trip to Hong Kong. On that airplane to China, in between glasses of cheap Cabernet, I picked up the in-flight magazine and began flipping through it. I saw a full-page advertisement for a major hotel chain in Hong Kong. The ad appealed to me because it touted how this hotel chain is known for having the very best and most comfortable *pillows* of any hotel chain. Since I'm a super fan of fine pillows, the ad got my attention.

As soon as I arrived in Hong Kong, I walked through the airport and saw a large billboard advertisement. It featured a woman who looked like me resting her head on a luxurious-looking pillow. I saw in the corner of the billboard the same hotel chain's logo. The ad copy read, "Our hotels have the finest pillows in Asia." Score!

I thought, "There's a girl who looks like me. She likes

pillows like me. She's staying in the hotel chain with the comfy pillows." After I went through customs, I collected my luggage. Then I saw a rack of printed brochures for hotels and attractions in Hong Kong. I scoured the rack for the brochure of that hotel with the world-famous comfy pillows; I found it and opened it up. Sure enough, there on the brochure was that same girl who looks like me. The brochure had even more information on the pillows.

At this point, it's obvious—I was completely sold on the CPH (Comfy Pillow Hotel).

I immediately called and switched my reservation to the CPH. That advert in the airport, the in-flight magazine, and the printed brochure really worked on me. I couldn't wait to lay my head on those famous pillows and drift off to sleep.

When I walked into my room at the Comfy Pillow Hotel, I immediately belly-flopped on the bed. I was ready for a deep sleep, just like I get on my pillows at home. I reached over and felt those hotel pillows with joyous anticipation. And then...

Massive disappointment hit.

Were the pillows awful? Meh. They weren't *horrible*. But

I've had much, much better. What irked me was that the pillows did not live up to what was promised in the advertisements. Not even close. It was a bait and switch. It was especially disappointing after I went through the trouble to change my reservation *just* so I could sleep on better pillows.

Those advertisements were *the reason* I stayed in that hotel. I wondered why the NSCPH (Not So Comfy Pillow Hotel) ran those misleading ads if they *knew* they had the same lame pillows that every other hotel chain had. I suppose the marketing department probably did some research that international travellers suffer from stiff necks. So, they launched their ad campaign around pillows. But without actually spending money on premium pillows, it was just marketing.

FAST-FORWARD TO TODAY

Now fast-forward to the present day. I once again was going to Hong Kong on a business trip. In the intervening years, consumer habits had changed dramatically. This time I didn't rely on advertising to help me decide which hotel to stay in.

I didn't even look at advertising.

Instead, I looked on TripAdvisor. Did you know you can

search pillow reviews on TripAdvisor? With about four clicks I was reading hundreds of reviews about hotel pillows in Hong Kong. It turns out there are thousands of business travellers who are also pillow connoisseurs just like me. The consensus was that the hotel I had stayed in ten years earlier, the NSCPH, is *not* known for having fine pillows. In fact, the opposite is true; reviewers were *hating* on their pillows.

Then I learned that a different international hotel chain was getting rave reviews for their pillows. I checked out a few dozen reviews about that hotel chain in general and the Hong Kong property in particular. That's where I booked my reservation, and that's how I made my decision.

BURN ME ONCE, SHAME ON YOU

Coincidentally, on my flight to Hong Kong a few weeks later, I opened the in-flight magazine and once again saw a full-page ad for the Not So Comfy Pillow Hotel I stayed in a decade earlier. But this time I had already done my research. I thought to myself, "Nope. I have a lot more information now. I know better. Those ads won't fool me again."

In the airport I saw more advertisements for the NSCPH. I snarled at them and kept walking. I did not for one second believe their advertising. I believed the more than one hundred user reviews I had read online. Even if the CEO of that hotel chain was standing in the airport and telling me how comfortable his pillows are from a megaphone flanked by beautiful promo girls, I would not believe it. I would not be made a fool again.

LOGO PLACEMENT DOESN'T HAVE A PRAYER

This changes everything. Consumers have so much more information available to them, which influences their purchase behaviour. They equally hate being made a fool of. The reality today is that advertising not only doesn't resonate, but it's almost consciously *ignored* in isolation.

The way consumers make decisions to shop, buy, and spend money today is light years from the way they did it ten or twenty years ago. So much more information is available with just a few taps on a mobile screen. It's so easy to access reviews, tweets, snaps, and in-depth product information. All consumer purchasing has changed in this way. It's a profound shift in behaviour.

The takeaway from the Hong Kong pillow story is this. In the Information Age, not even expensive advertising campaigns with huge billboards, TV ads, magazine ads, and million-pound budgets work well anymore. Which begs the following question.

So how well do you think just putting a logo on something works?

Placing a logo and hoping it will be enough to influence buying decisions is futile. Logo placement worked well ten or twenty years ago, but it just does not work anymore. Consumers are far too sophisticated and informed for that. You're a consumer, so you know this is true from your own experience.

Information is everywhere, and it's so easy to access. Consumers now seek information before parting with their money. That means brands have to do better. No matter how clever and well-known their logo is, brands are finding that pure logo-placement sponsorship deals have lost much of their value.

CONSUMERS IGNORE MOST ADS

This represents a tectonic shift in the consumer advertising industry. Not only are paid ads and logos ineffective, but if online user reviews contradict what the ads say, consumers think the advertiser is lying. If consumers lose trust, they will likely never become a customer.

It's to the point now that consumers ignore most advertisements altogether. They utilise their own credible sources of information to make purchase decisions, and they know how to find it in less than fifteen seconds.

The pillow story is tremendously important in terms of the way brands need to start thinking about what is valuable to them through a sponsorship campaign and assets. This is also important for rights holders in terms of the assets they offer. If sponsorship is supposed to be mutually beneficial, giving a brand a logo placement won't benefit the brand, because it won't generate ROI. Since we're all consumers, we know this from our own experience. When is the last time you even *noticed* a logo?

Yet remarkably, logo-placement deals still make up the majority of sponsorship.

IMPORTANT DEFINITIONS

The terms below can have many definitions, of course; but here is what they mean in the context of this book and in the world of sponsorship.

Rights Holder: Any company or organisation that is *seeking* a sponsor.

Sponsor: Any company or organisation that purchases sponsorship rights. Sometimes I'll substitute the word *brand* for sponsor, because brands are often the ones who purchase sponsorship rights.

Audience: The people who will interact with the activity, whether off-line or online.

Assets: The rights that rights holders sell to brands for a certain period of time.

Activation: The use of the rights holder's assets, typically for marketing purposes.

Sponsorship Sales Agency: An agency that helps rights holders understand and value their assets, and then sells them to brands in the form of a sponsorship agreement.

Activation Agency: A marketing agency that helps brands find creative ways to utilise their sponsorship rights.

HAVE A COKE AND A SMILE

The old rule of sponsorship is to slap a logo on something

and get paid for it. Coca-Cola was famous for this. For decades, their logo has been ubiquitous, because they sponsored just about everything at one time or another. The Coca-Cola sponsorship strategy in the 1980s was summed up with, "We like your shit, so please drink our shit." People saw the Coke logo and associated it with fun and having a good time. Basic brand recall. For a long time, it worked.

Not anymore. Coke's strategy has changed, because the world has changed. Slapping a Coke logo on everything no longer delivers meaningful ROI.

AUDIENCES ARE ACCESSIBLE EVERYWHERE

The proliferation of information platforms and publishers has further eroded the value of traditional logo-placement sponsorship deals. Years ago, the only way to reach sports fans was to sponsor sporting events, teams, or stadiums, or to advertise on sports broadcasts.

Placing a Budweiser beer logo on the scoreboard at a football game worked great. If brands wanted to reach women, they would advertise on TV shows and in magazines that were consumed by women. To reach teens and young people, you would go through schools or universities.

Now there are a myriad of media outlets, online influencers, and content creators, including bloggers, Instagrammers, Twitter trendsetters, niche websites, vloggers, YouTubers, Facebook Live stars, Pinterest mavens, Snapchatters, Twitch gamers, brand journalists, digital news outlets, thought leaders, and so on. There are content publishers and influencers for any and every interest. Where there used to be a few dozen magazines for mothers, now there are thousands of parenting blogs tailored to every demographic and interest within the parenting segment. Football fans can now follow thousands of different content publishers, hundreds of which might be dedicated just to their favourite team, and dozens of which might be dedicated just to their favourite player. Brands no longer have to rely on putting their logo on a football stadium or ESPN to reach football fans.

Audiences are accessible everywhere.

Influencers who have a specialty in one area can often cut across demographics. YouTube star PewDiePie built an audience of millions by playing video games. Gamers will spend hours watching PewDiePie's content and engaging with him in multiple ways. If you want to reach teens and young adults, you no longer have to go through schools; you can reach them through PewDiePie. For a brand trying to reach teens, which do you think works better: paying to put their logo on milk cartons at the school cafeteria, or forming a partnership with PewDiePie to create original sponsored content that he will promote to his 53 million subscribers totalling 14 billion video views?

MEASURING SUCCESS

I recently spoke to the chairman of a global insurance and retail conglomerate. I told him what I do and asked how his current sponsorship programmes with a premier footfall club were going. I specifically asked how many new insurance policies they had sold from their involvement. He looked confused and asked, "What do you mean? That sponsorship gets our logo in front of seven million people." I said, "But do you know how much new business that has resulted in?" He had no idea, nor did he seem to think it mattered.

Imagine that; a major corporation spending tens of millions of pounds to place their logo on a football stadium without even the foggiest clue if they were getting any benefit from it. Who cares if your logo is seen by millions of fans? So what? You have to measure what that exposure is getting you. If you haven't converted any of those millions of fans into customers, it's all a big waste of money.

Worse yet, if those seven million fans are already your

customers and your sponsorship objective is to generate increased revenue from a different target market, you will utterly fail. I'm amazed that financially conservative business executives will try to save money and obsess over the bottom line in every other area of their business, but are profligate when spending money on sponsorship.

There are much better, more effective, and measurable ways to spend money on marketing and brand building. For example, what would happen if a sponsor took the same amount of money they previously spent on putting their logo on the Liverpool Football Club and instead spent it on a savvy digital influencer campaign specifically designed to reach their precise target market and convert them into customers?

Not only would that digital campaign drive actual revenue, but it would also track customers and purchases through the sales funnel so the brand would know precisely what their ROI is on every dollar spent. Compare that to the vague and unquantifiable benefit of having football fans simply see a logo on a stadium.

THE INDUSTRY IS CHANGING

There is a trend of prestigious brands pulling back from traditional badging sponsorships with renewed scrutiny and accountability for where their sponsorship spend is going. This is happening because rights holders aren't giving brands the assets they need to work in the type of environment where consumers have access to instant information.

In 2013, after seven years of being the title sponsor of the McLaren Formula One team, Vodafone announced their sponsorship would end. It was a moment that shocked the sports world *and* the sponsorship industry. By some reports, that Vodafone sponsorship deal was worth up to £50 million per year to McLaren. It was primarily a badging exercise, with Vodafone logos on the cars, team uniforms, pit stop, and so on.

News reports stated that Vodafone decided to end the sponsorship "following a review of marketing strategy." Vodafone's chief commercial officer issued this statement: "Our brand is evolving, and we've concluded we will have less of a need for this kind of exposure in the future." Code for, "Slapping our logo on cars isn't worth £50 million per year, because everyone is already familiar with Vodafone."

ENGAGE CUSTOMERS WHERE THEY ARE

Instead of spending all that money on logo placement, or sponsoring a different sport, Vodafone decided to reach their customers where those customers engage with content. Vodafone has copious amounts of data on where their customers are and how their customers want to engage with them. They know how their brand can be influential to their customer base. Formula One clearly was no longer working. So Vodafone pulled money away from traditional badging sponsorships and TV ads and used it to create an online content experience called Vodafone Firsts.

Vodafone Firsts is their own proprietary, content-led, data-driven, user-generated online hub. Vodafone prides itself on being an innovative company that has achieved a lot of "firsts." Keeping with that theme, they built Vodafone Firsts around the idea of people doing innovative things, achieving firsts, or doing something for the first time.

Vodafone chose this strategy because they wanted to reach a wider demographic than just Formula One fans. Women, teens, millennials, seniors, creatives, and many other groups can all identify with innovation and doing something for the first time; but they aren't necessarily the typical audience for motorsports like Formula One.

BRANDS CREATING THEIR OWN DEALS

The North Face customers are outdoors-type people. The brand's challenge is that outdoor people are hard to reach—they aren't home on the couch in front of the TV, or watching sports, or on their computers. They're also into different types of outdoor activities, including everything from yoga and mountain biking to skiing and rock climbing.

The North Face struggled to find an effective platform that targeted their diverse customer portfolio. So rather than trying to *find* them, they built something to *attract* them. They created their own event and in so doing became their own rights holder.

The North Face launched The North Face Night Ray Outdoor Festival in 2015. It offered a wide range of adventure activities, including workshops and classes with The North Face athletes and climbers, musical performances, and lectures by adventurers and explorers. Of course, The North Face products were front and centre throughout the entire event. So instead of sponsoring a bunch of different events that *sort of* reached various pockets of their ideal audience of potential customers, The North Face created their own event that *perfectly* targeted their ideal customers.

Cleverly, they took it one step further. To spread the costs and reduce expense, they went out and found other like-minded outdoorsy brands that had the same challenge reaching that elusive outdoor customer base. Jeep became the cosponsor of the festival.

There are some important things to point out in both the Vodafone and The North Face examples. First, they're creating new models of sponsorship. Second, in both cases, the brand becomes not just the sponsor, but also the rights holder. So, the brand has full control over both the assets *and* the creative. This is a tremendous benefit to the brand, and one borne out of necessity.

SUCCESSFUL SPONSORSHIP REQUIRES ASKING QUESTIONS

One of the challenges to doing sponsorship well is knowing the right questions to ask. Harder yet for most is to actually ask them. Even at that stage, people fail to listen to the answer. Always ask the rights holders and/or the brands you're working with what their ideal partner looks like. Ask them how they want to work with that partner. Ask them to describe exactly what their objectives are. Make them commit in writing to specific goals, and then agree upon what the metrics will be for determining if those goals are achieved. All parties should buy in to those metrics.

Sadly, many people working in this field just don't put in

the required effort. That leads to brands and rights holders making poor decisions based on gut instincts instead of data. Sponsorship is often infused with a lot of passion. That's a good thing. But that passion has to be tempered with analytical thinking and data.

REMINDER: IMPORTANT TAKEAWAYS

CHAPTER 1 TAKEAWAY: Consumers ignore most ads. So if your marketing strategy is built only upon traditional advertising, you're wasting a lot of money for diminishing returns.

CHAPTER 2 TAKEAWAY:

CHAPTER 3 TAKEAWAY:

CHAPTER 4 TAKEAWAY:

CHAPTER 5 TAKEAWAY:

CHAPTER 6 TAKEAWAY:

CHAPTER TWO

DON'T MAKE IT ABOUT YOU

My palms were sweating. My heart was racing. I wasn't just nervous—I was petrified. The stakes were high. If I failed, it would be devastating.

The statue of Mahatma Gandhi zoomed by me in a blur. Or rather, I zoomed by it. The bright flowers adorning its pedestal splashed red and yellow across my periphery. I was dashing through Tavistock Square as fast as my pumps would carry me. Briefcase in one hand, box of proposals in the other. Little did I know that those proposals would lead me to one of the most important light-bulb moments in my career.

I passed the cherry tree dedicated to the victims of the atomic-bomb blasts in Hiroshima and Nagasaki. I passed the bust of Virginia Woolf, one of my favourite English writers; despite having no formal training, Woolf taught herself to write and became one of the most renowned and respected writers of the twentieth century.

When I reached my destination, the BMA House, I paused to catch my breath. The enormous brick building was not just impressive—it was imposing. I looked past the century-old wrought-iron Gates of Remembrance to the clock above. I sighed and thought to myself, "As usual, way ahead of time."

I was about to conduct a full-day private training session for staff members at a prestigious and world-renowned medical journal. I knew they had impossibly high standards and great expectations. I had to be at the top of my game today. There was no other option.

One of my character traits, or flaws depending on how you view it, is my coping mechanism for fear, which is to absolutely overprepare by a factor of ten. Maybe twenty. I spent hours and hours researching for this presentation and many more hours rehearsing it. I knew I was ready, but I still felt intense anxiety.

This was only the second sponsorship boot camp I'd ever

done. It was the first full-day event. The previous boot camp I did was only a half-day session. A boot camp is our agency's version of a one-day practical training session to download everything we know about sponsorship. We have two types:

1. We work with an organisation that is seeking sponsors to create a winning sponsorship strategy, identify and value their assets, revamp their pitch, build their ideal target list, and get them ready to take their pitch to market and hopefully secure a sponsor.
2. We work with a brand to inspire their teams to think both creatively and commercially about the rights they are about to purchase or have already purchased.

It's a big job, and it happens all in one day, so it has to be good. When I walked into the medical journal offices in the BMA House, I was anxious, on edge, and tense. I was so nervous that I nearly forgot my own name at the reception desk when checking in.

I'll continue this story in a moment, but first I need to set the stage with a few definitions and concepts. As Virginia Woolf once said, "Thought and theory must precede all salutary action."

TURNING AN AIRCRAFT CARRIER

One of my goals is to change the traditional thinking about sponsorship. But since the same old thinking and processes have been around for so long, they're difficult to change. When companies, rights holders, and agencies have been doing sponsorship the same way decade after decade, it's hard to think in new and different ways. It's just plain easier to do what's been done many times before. Nobody's going to get fired for doing what the last person did, right?

Trying to change the way brands and rights holders approach sponsorship is like trying to turn an aircraft carrier; it takes time. But there is a more effective way. If the only concept you grasp in this entire book is the one in this chapter, it will catapult you to entirely new levels of success in sponsorship.

Once I learned and understood the concept in this chapter, it changed my career and put me on the path to success. It happened in a light-bulb moment early in my career. It was one of those moments when everything changed for me. I was struck with a crystal-clear realisation that has influenced and guided everything I've done in sponsorship since. As I hope it will for you.

And the best part? The concept is incredibly simple. Yet,

oddly, when we try to teach this new trick to people who have worked their entire careers in the sponsorship industry, they don't get it. Or at least they act like they don't get it, because they don't want to do the extra work that's involved.

☀ IT'S NOT ABOUT YOU!

Through our sponsorship training and boot camps, along with individual consulting sessions, we've worked with literally thousands of clients, brands, and rights holders. We see the same mistakes over and over again. First among those mistakes is the inclination of the organisation seeking a sponsor to *talk all about themselves.*

> **REMEMBER THESE FOUR WORDS**
>
> It's not about you!

For example, let's say a museum is planning their big annual fundraiser, and they're looking for a title sponsor. They begin approaching companies and brands that they know spend sponsorship dollars. They send out hundreds of beautifully produced PowerPoint presentations with lots of photos, charts, and pictures of people enjoying the museum. They lecture the reader about how great the museum is, how all of their exhibits are unique, and why the museum is a priceless gem and a community treasure. It never occurs to them that they just spent forty-five minutes of the one-hour meeting talking about themselves.

What marketing brand managers *really* want to know is this: "How will sponsoring your event help *us?*"

Talking about ourselves is a natural human tendency that we all have. No one knows more about you than you. You're an expert on you. Similarly, you know your business or nonprofit really well too. You work there every day. You understand the organisation's culture. You know about the work it does. You're proud of the impact your organisation is having in the world. And since you're so knowledgeable, you could talk about it for hours.

In contrast, you don't necessarily know much about the strategies of the brands you're looking to sign as a sponsor. You don't work for the brand. You don't know their staff, their executives, their vision, or their mission. It's just easier to stay in your comfort zone and talk about what you do know, especially when you're trying to convince people to give you money.

Unfortunately, this doesn't work.

It's not about you. That's the key concept of this chapter. It's that simple. Ah, but what exactly does that mean in the context of sponsorship? My story about the prestigious medical journal will illustrate this point vividly.

I WAS A NERVOUS WRECK

When I walked into the medical journal offices in the BMA House, I was so nervous that my mouth went completely dry. I felt like a nervous wreck, and I'm sure I looked like one too. I was doing my best to keep it together.

When I was greeted by the medical journal's team, they were lovely—warm, welcoming, and so nice that I instantly felt more at ease. They were a small team, only three people. But they had successfully brought on several major sponsors for their awards programme, and they had secured hundreds of thousands of pounds in sponsorship revenue, which was an achievement in its own right. They were extremely sharp and experienced at sponsorship. They had reached out to us simply because they wanted to grow their sponsorship revenue even bigger. I got set up and began.

One of the ways I like to help clients understand sponsorship is by showing them dozens of proposals prepared by a wide variety of organisations that are seeking sponsors.

Over the years, I've collected thousands of sponsorship proposals from different industry sectors. Approximately 99.9 percent of them are bad. Most are actually terrible. I'm not exaggerating.

The question I always start this particular boot camp segment with is this: "Based on any of these proposals, would you give this person money? Why or why not?" It's fascinating because even though they don't know anything about the industries or the platforms in the proposals they evaluate, instinctively and quickly they tell you why they think it's valuable or not. They can even accurately identify what the problems are in each proposal. To my surprise, I've never once had anyone say, "I'm not equipped to evaluate this."

This is a valuable exercise because it gives a buyer's perspective. Rights holders always think about things only from a seller's perspective. So it's helpful to look at it from a buyer's perspective.

Ironically, in most of my boot camps when the group criticises a proposal for doing something wrong, I say, "You're right. But *your* proposal is doing the exact same thing. You're making the same mistake." It's a real eye-opener for them to realise how quick they are to judge, but don't expect the same judgment on them.

THE COVER PHOTO I'LL NEVER FORGET

After discussing all these other proposals, I asked the medical journal team to show me their proposal. At first glance, I was impressed.

It was quite nice looking, and they had clearly put a lot of time and effort into it. The first thing that struck me was the cover photo. It was a big, bold image of the medical journal's CEO. I had never seen her before. I had no idea who she was. I assumed she must be well-known in that community. Her photo was featured so prominently that I assumed she must have cured some dreadful disease or done something huge in medicine.

When I opened the proposal, I saw another smaller picture of the CEO surrounded by paragraphs upon paragraphs of text that literally filled the page. It was a rather lengthy essay from the CEO all about the journal, what the organisation stands for, and why it's important. On the next page were details of the event they were seeking sponsorship for, and the fourth page described the journal's key assets.

MY LIGHT-BULB MOMENT

There was *not one word* devoted to answering the question of how sponsoring the event would benefit the sponsors. The entire proposal was designed to show off how exceptional the journal is and how amazing their CEO is. She most certainly is, but that's not what brands care about.

I really wanted to understand the thought process behind putting the CEO on the cover. I said to the group, "Is your CEO famous?" They sort of shrugged and said, "No. Not really."

"Did she save the world by eradicating some disease or inventing a new medicine?" No.

"Did she walk on the moon?" No.

"Has she been featured in the news or earned lots of publicity?" No.

"Will her photo and her name resonate with brands and draw the interest of potential sponsors?" Not really, no.

"Then why is she on the front cover of the proposal?"

The room went quiet. It was an awkward moment of silence. They all looked at one another, then back at me, then smiled uncomfortably, and looked down.

I think we were all hoping someone would rescue us by

bursting into the room with tea and chocolate biscuits, or a bottle of Johnnie Walker Blue Label. Hell, in that moment, even Johnnie Walker Red Label would do.

It became apparent that no one at the medical journal had even *considered* whether the CEO was the right person to feature in the organisation's sponsorship pitch.

They hadn't given it a single thought.

At that moment, a light bulb went on, for all of us. It was obvious that everyone was thinking the same thing: "Why *is* she on the front cover?"

This is a classic example of how even experienced sponsorship veterans build out entire pitches without ever thinking about the most important person—*the buyer*. What does the *buyer* need? Potential sponsors don't know who this medical journal CEO is, and they don't need to. Nor do they care to learn every highlight of the one-hundred-year history of the publication.

Sure, they want to be comfortable that the organisation is well-respected and legit. Beyond that, they have only one concern: "What's in it for us?"

What's stunning is that no one had ever raised the question

of whether or not to put the CEO on the cover. Someone made the decision to put her there and then padded that decision with enough copy to bore anyone to death. It was clearly done without any thought about whether that would appeal to potential partners.

Was there another, *better* option? It turns out there was.

LIKE TINDER DATES, MARKETING MANAGERS ONLY CARE ABOUT ONE THING

This is an incredibly common phenomenon, both in sponsorship and in the world as a whole. Opportunities are missed every day because the team doing the pitching focuses on *themselves*, instead of focusing on whom they're pitching to. That would be like going on a first date and showing up late, drunk, wearing your pyjamas, and then talking nonstop about yourself for two hours. You hopefully wouldn't do that if you wanted to get a second date.

Except this is worse. Because finding a sponsor is an essential source of revenue for many organisations, especially nonprofits. People's jobs and livelihoods depend on it.

Do brand managers really care to read a one-thousand-word essay about the CEO? If the CEO is Warren Buffett or Rupert Murdoch, then yes. Otherwise, no. Do they want to know that the CEO serves on the board of six charities? No. Will they read and study the organisation's in-depth mission statement? Unlikely.

This is not job-specific; everyone is busy, so make your point fast. People will understand your organisation's mission in thirty seconds. "We get it: you save children in Africa. Now why should we sponsor you?"

The chances are slim that an overworked brand representative will take the time to study a sponsorship proposal that never clearly articulates what's in it for them.

SO COMMON IT'S CRINGEWORTHY

The story of this medical journal's sponsorship proposal is just one example of thousands. It's a microcosm of the entire sponsorship industry. I've seen the same mistake made by some of the best and brightest executives and agency heads. They believe deeply that the work they're doing is important, and they want to tell brands about it in detail. That's very noble. But brands simply don't care.

More and more professionals in the sponsorship industry are starting to realise the folly of this mistake. Yet they're still doing it! Why? Because it's easy to talk about yourself, but it's hard to talk to a potential sponsor about their specific needs, goals, and challenges. To have that conversation intelligently, you have to do your homework. You have to study the potential sponsor. You have to put in the time to learn about them and their needs. You should understand the DNA of that brand *before* you walk into that pitch meeting.

IS THAT HUGH GRANT?

The funny kicker to the medical journal story is that five pages into the sponsorship proposal was a picture of the movie star Hugh Grant. He was photographed at one of the medical journal's events. I was intrigued.

"Why was Hugh Grant at your event?"

"He's one of our supporters."

"Does that mean he likes your journal and he supports your events?"

"Yes, he'll do whatever we ask of him."

"Whaaaaaaaaaat?"

Now I really needed a glass of Johnnie Walker Blue. A double.

I said, "Let me get this straight. One of the most famous actors in the world is a supporter of your organisation, yet instead of putting Hugh Grant on the cover of your sponsorship proposal, you used a picture of your CEO whom no one has ever heard of? Did it not occur to you that featuring Hugh Grant prominently could help attract big sponsors?"

Silence.

Is Hugh Grant fundamentally important to the medical journal? Of course not. But his picture at last year's fundraiser is an attention-grabber that should go on the proposal cover. It will pique the interest of potential sponsors and lead to a positive opening conversation. It's absolutely vital to provide potential sponsors with an experience of emotional resonance immediately. Otherwise, there's a high chance your sponsorship proposal will be filed in the trash bin.

After the full-day boot camp, the medical journal redesigned their sponsorship proposal and pitch materials. They focused on how their sponsorship would strategically help a brand achieve its goals and why. They analytically identified the types of brands that would most benefit from sponsoring the journal. They continued their past sponsorship successes, and even expanded their sponsorship programme by selling assets to new brands.

CAUTION: CELEBRITIES

It's important to recognise that putting a celebrity on the cover isn't always a good idea. Please don't read this and think that calling Hugh Grant will solve all your sponsorship problems. It won't. When working with celebrities, I usually prefer to keep them off the front cover of proposals, because the focus of the materials is on the wider opportunity. Hugh Grant was a good fit for the medical journal because he was already a supporter, and because his popularity presented the organisation and what many would deem "yet another boring black-tie gala" in a younger, livelier light.

DO YOUR HOMEWORK

Spending most of a sponsorship pitch meeting talking about yourself is not a good strategy. Trying to connect with the motivations of other people is difficult to do. You run the risk of making a mistake and looking foolish.

The solution is to do your homework and study the brand. This takes time and effort. Brands are not hiding their strategies. They *want* you to know what they are trying to sell, who their customers are, and what their brand stands for. That's what drives their sales and their brand identity. You'll find a wealth of information usually right on their website. Read their information online, watch their content on YouTube, study their blog, and watch their videos. Go to the company's "Press and Media" page and read all their press releases. Again, this isn't hard, but it takes more time than doing nothing.

After you've done your research, you'll have a solid understanding of the brand and their strategy. Of course, you won't know everything, but you'll know enough to talk about *them* and *their* needs. Understand that you can't know everything, but don't be afraid to make an informed guess about their priorities. You may sometimes be wrong, but if you've taken the time to do your research, that rarely happens.

Once you start this conversation, be sure to ask plenty of questions. You can't learn everything from doing research before the meeting. It's always best to ask key questions to make sure you really understand the organisation and what their goals are. Ask what the brand is hoping to accomplish with their sponsorship budget. What are their specific objectives? Ask them how well their past sponsorships have worked, and how they measure success. Ask what they would do differently and why. You can even ask why they are interested in your specific sponsorship proposal.

Most people never ask the basic questions. It's usually for fear of looking foolish. It's not embarrassing to ask questions; it should be a conversation.

Once you take time to do some research, it's amazing how easy it is to find out what other organisations are looking for, and to speak to them in a knowledgeable way that will attract their attention. By asking the right questions, you are more likely to understand their needs and thus secure the right sponsorship. Truly understanding their needs is the only way to achieve a mutually beneficial partnership in which both sponsor and rights holder achieve their objectives.

MUTUAL BENEFIT OR EMPTY TALK?

Almost everyone who sells sponsorship rights talks the language of "mutual benefit." "There will be plenty of mutual benefit if Barclays sponsors our beauty pageant." It's a great concept. Everyone can agree that mutual benefit is a worthy goal. Unfortunately, the actions often fail to match the words. People who promote the concept of mutual benefit too often sell sponsorship rights that have little to no value for the people purchasing them.

Rights holders and brands that are locked into unproductive relationships are like two people stuck in a bad marriage. Both would be better served by dissolving the partnership and forging new relationships with partners who suit their needs better. If your business isn't a good partner for your current brand or rights holder, you're not only holding yourself back—you're also holding *them* back.

SQUARE PEGS DON'T FIT IN ROUND HOLES

Always start by asking what will resonate with the people you want to reach. If you do that, you're much more likely to choose good partners and approach them intelligently. Instead of asking, "Who has money, and how can we get that money?" consider which brands would actually *benefit* most from entering into a partnership with you.

These early decisions are critical to your success. When you try to force a square peg into a round hole, it just doesn't work. A sponsorship designed just to get money from a brand will be rejected and will likely not get a sponsor to commit. If you don't get a sponsor, you will have wasted all the time and resources you invested. You would have been better off not seeking a sponsor at all. Sponsorship is not money for nothing; don't confuse it with a charitable donation.

SPONSORSHIP VS. PARTNERSHIP

My biggest pet peeve is when sponsorship salespeople say, "We don't do sponsorships; we do *partnerships*. A partnership is better because it means we're working together." The implication is that calling it a "partnership" somehow makes it *more* mutually beneficial than if it was *only* a sponsorship. Nonsense! You don't change the nature of something just by calling it by a different name.

In my opinion, in the world of sponsorship, these two words—sponsorship and partnership—are the same. Both involve working collaboratively to achieve a result that wouldn't be possible by working independently. I use the two words interchangeably, because in this line of work, they represent the same thing.

SELECTIVE BREEDING

When you stop thinking about only what *you* want out of a partnership, and instead think about what your partners want, you open up new and different conversations. Even if the first people you approach don't make good partners, new opportunities will appear when you change your mindset.

Happy sponsors breed more sponsorships. When a deliberately targeted sponsor does a significant campaign and generates a solid ROI on it, they tell their friends, colleagues, and suppliers. Soon, their friends and colleagues ask to be part of the same sponsorship platform. This has happened with so many of our clients.

If you start by focusing on your own needs, watch the doors close. If you start by thinking strategically about the client's needs, watch doors open. This isn't idealism. It's pragmatism.

REMINDER: IMPORTANT TAKEAWAYS

Succeeding at sponsorship does not happen by following just one or two of the principles in this book. It requires all of them.

CHAPTER 1 TAKEAWAY: Consumers ignore most ads. So if your marketing strategy is built only upon traditional advertising, you're wasting a lot of money for diminishing returns.

CHAPTER 2 TAKEAWAY: When trying to sell sponsorship, do not focus on yourself or your organisation. *Focus on the sponsor.* By asking the right questions, you are likely to understand their needs and thus secure the right sponsorship.

CHAPTER 3 TAKEAWAY:

CHAPTER 4 TAKEAWAY:

CHAPTER 5 TAKEAWAY:

CHAPTER 6 TAKEAWAY:

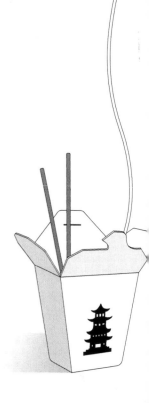

CHAPTER THREE

IT'S NOT ABOUT WHAT *YOU* NEED

The thick layer of straw that covered the wooden platform was there to absorb the blood. About two hundred spectators waited patiently for the gruesome show to begin. Wearing a black hood to conceal his face, the executioner entered the courtyard. He was holding an enormous axe, the ragged steel blade glinting in the afternoon sun. An ominous sign of the times, the hickory axe handle appeared well-worn; it had clearly seen plenty of use.

Guards led the gaunt-looking convicted criminal up to greet his towering executioner. It was customary for the victim to pay a small gratuity to his own executioner and to forgive him for what was about to happen. The sincerest hope of the damned was that the executioner's blade would strike the soft flesh of the neck strong and true, bringing death swiftly, if not painlessly. But that was not always the case.

Death by beheading was a horrifying ordeal for the more than one hundred victims who met their end at the dreaded Tower of London. If the executioner was tired, careless, or—God forbid—drunk, multiple swings could be required to completely sever the head from the body. The Countess of Salisbury suffered eleven blows from the executioner's axe before she perished.

The Tower of London was the most feared building in England for nearly one thousand years. Countless prisoners and enemies of the state were imprisoned and tortured there. William the Conqueror had the ominous fortress built in 1078. Starting in 1100, it began operation as a prison, though that was not all it was used for. It still held prisoners as recently as 1952. The last person to be executed there was Josef Jakobs, a German spy captured during World War II.

Today, the world-famous Tower of London is a UNESCO World Heritage Site. It's a symbol of English history and power. And it's a museum housing some of the most incredible and fascinating exhibits in Europe.

MY PRIVATE INVITATION TO THE TOWER OF LONDON

Around the time of the London Olympics, I received a call from representatives of the Queen. Yes, the Queen of England. They were exploring sponsorship opportunities for some of their assets. They asked me to come value one of their exhibits, the Crown Jewels exhibit at the Tower of London.

An organisation called Historic Royal Palaces, or the HRP, manages and maintains many of the Queen's properties. These include the Tower of London, the Crown Jewels, Kensington Palace, Hillsborough Castle, and others.

The HRP were seeking a sponsor for the exhibit, and they were offering to let a company or brand put their name on the exhibit as a title sponsor, in exchange for a fee. I went to meet with them at the Tower of London where the Crown Jewels reside under lock and key.

Three stylish HRP executives greeted me in the reception area. They were all impeccably dressed in classic Savile Row suits and freshly shined John Lobb wingtip leather shoes. I could smell the shoe polish. Each one had perfectly coiffed hair with not a strand out of place. I got the distinct impression that these were top HRP executives, the best of the best, and there was no doubt that they represented the Queen's interests with utter professionalism and pride. Clearly nothing was left to chance. I was impressed, and I am not easily impressed.

They took me on a private tour of the Tower of London and the Crown Jewels exhibit. As we walked through the halls, I was struck by the deep sense of pride the HRP has in the rich history of the English Crown and the House of Windsor.

The jewels sparkled and danced in the custom lighting. It was an elegant blur of sovereign crowns, consort crowns, ornate swords, sceptres, rings, orbs, altar plates, and more. The jewels are a shining, dazzling, historic representation of eight hundred years of English monarchy.

The entire experience was first-class. It was breathtaking, really. I was in awe.

I was also struck by the amount of planning and effort my hosts had gone through to welcome me in such an unforgettable way. They had thought of everything. It was clear to me that the amount of specific intent evident in their preparation for my visit was encompassed in everything they did. I was sure that they were equally adroit when it came to running their sponsorships. I was familiar with the HRP, and I knew they had a history of successful sponsorships.

I thought, "These people know what they're doing."

THEY LURED ME INTO A DUNGEON

I asked them to tell me more about what they were trying to accomplish through sponsorship. I asked what their goals were, and if they had ever worked with an agency before. They said they had never worked with an agency, and they had never received a professional evaluation of what their sponsorship opportunity was actually worth.

They took me to a plush conference room where they showed me their sponsorship proposal. It was the most elegant document I have ever seen. That's saying a lot, because my team and I see ten thousand proposals each year. The HRP team had their proposal printed on very expensive parchment paper, it was embossed, and it was filled with gorgeous images. "Elegance befitting royalty," I thought. "These people are *good*. Finally, a team of sponsorship professionals who really gets it. They understand sponsorship."

Or so I thought.

HERE COMES THE EXECUTIONER

When I got to the last page of the proposal, I read that

the value of the sponsorship they were seeking was a very specific number. For the sake of example, let's just say it was £872,450. I was confused. They were asking for a very specific amount, yet they told me earlier that they had never had the sponsorship valued by an agency.

With a puzzled look on my face, I asked, "So you have in fact had this valued then, right?"

"No, we have not."

"You never had an agency tell you what your sponsorship is worth?"

"Never."

Hmmm. Usually when an organisation doesn't know what their sponsorship value is, they ask for a round number, like £800,000 or £1 million. Yet the HRP were asking for exactly £872,450. I knew there must be a reason.

"So how did you come up with £872,450, as a very precise number?"

"That's the amount of money we need to pay for the renovation of one of our corridors down the hall."

"Wait. I'm sorry, what?"

It took a moment for that to sink in. Then I understood. I was both amused and frustrated at the same time. Amused because it struck me as hilarious that the amount of money they *needed* to pay for an unrelated construction bill was the *value* they placed on their sponsorship. I also found it funny that they were totally open and obvious about it, as in, "Well, of course, it's something else that we need money for." It was as if it was the most natural, matter-of-fact thing in the world.

I was also frustrated. Because *this is how everybody does sponsorship*. I've seen it thousands of times. It's not only wrong—it goes against all common sense.

OFF WITH MY HEAD

The HRP combined two completely unrelated things. The value of their sponsorship benefits had absolutely nothing to do with the cost of their construction project. Yet inside that gorgeous, embossed proposal, they made them be the same thing. What frustrated me is that no one on their team thought it was odd in the least.

 This was another light-bulb moment for me. Even the Queen of England and her very experienced HRP sponsorship team didn't quite get it. This blew my mind. They failed to see that the assets they have to offer had an actual tangible, definable value to a sponsor. They saw sponsorship as a means to an end, rather than something that's going to provide value to a brand. Worse still, they failed to recognise that the sponsorship assets they were providing had any value to them at all.

Most organisations seeking a sponsor do the same thing. They create sponsorship packages based on their own needs, rather than on the value their assets provide to a brand. In many cases, they may not even know their assets even have value, and they may not understand they have to *provide value* to a brand in order to secure a sponsor.

They start with a figure based on how much money they need, and then they go out and try to sell a sponsorship for that amount. "We need £100,000 to fund our new swimming pool, so let's sell our sponsorship for £100,000." That's the way the industry has always been. But it's backwards, and it's problematic for a couple of reasons.

OVERPRICING AND UNDERPRICING ASSETS

There are two main ways this can end up badly. First, if an organisation prices their sponsorship *above* what it's really worth, they are likely to end up without a sponsor.

That can lead to budget shortfalls, event cancellations, and even layoffs.

The second way this can go badly is if they price their sponsorship *below* what it's worth. Then they are leaving money on the table. Neither of these two scenarios is ideal. But almost every organisation does this.

THE OPPORTUNITY COST OF OVERPRICING AND UNDERPRICING ASSETS

Here's an example of how costly it can be to overprice or underprice sponsorship assets. A popular series of running events in the UK holds more than fifteen different foot races all over the country each year. A combined one hundred thousand people participate in the races. For years, the series sold both local and national sponsorships ranging in price from £5,000 for a bronze-level sponsorship, up to £12,000 for a gold-level sponsorship, and £18,000 for naming rights.

Due to underpricing the bronze level, and overpricing the gold level, 80 percent of sponsors opted for bronze. This cost the event tens of thousands of pounds in lost revenue each year, and perhaps hundreds of thousands of pounds over the life of the series.

In the table, you can see how the bronze package has the highest ROI. For a sales price of £5,000 (row 19), the sponsor receives assets worth £17,810. That's an ROI greater than 250 percent. Compare that to the gold package, which is priced at £12,000 and offers a total value of £19,320. That's an ROI of only 60 percent.

ASSET PRICING TABLE

50,000 PEOPLE (18,000 RUNNERS)	NAMING RIGHTS	GOLD	SILVER	BRONZE	METHODOLOGY
Asset					
Naming rights of the 10K race					
Branding, logo, and link on the event website	£1,500	£1,500	£1,500	£450	Industry CPM based on impressions
Press release announcing partnership	£1,500	£1,500	£1,500	£1,500	Industry benchmark
Branding in the promotional flyers	£5,000	£5,000	£5,000	£5,000	Industry benchmark
Exhibition space in the Race Village	£7,700	£7,700	£7,700	£7,700	Local benchmark against exhibitions at events in the community
Branding on all event promotional material	£2,000	£800	£800	£800	Industry CPM based on direct mail rates
Start and finish branding	£80	£80	£80	£80	Industry CPM based on local billboard advertising
Branding throughout route	£200	£200	£200	£200	Industry CPM based on local billboard advertising
Complimentary race entries	£200	£100	£100	£100	Cost of entry
Branding on all event shirts and medal	£80	£80	£80	£80	Industry CPM based on local advertising
eShot to all entrants	£1,000	£1,000	£1,000	£1,000	Industry benchmark
Branding in all runners' communications	£100	£100	£100	£100	Industry CPM
Opportunity to include A5 within runner's packs	£460	£460	N	N	Industry CPM based on direct mail rates
Opportunity to provide promotional product in runner's packs	£800	£800	£800	£800	Industry CPM based on direct mail rates
Total Value	£20,620	£19,320	£18,860	£17,810	
Sales Price	£18,000	£12,000	£8,000	£5,000	
Inherent Savings	£2,620	£7,320	£10,860	£12,810	
Total Sponsors			1	4	
Total Sponsorship Received			£8,000	£25,000	

Why is there a higher ROI for the lowest-priced package (bronze) than the highest-priced package (gold)? It should be the other way around. Rights holders want sponsors to pay more, but to achieve that, they must provide high-value assets and price them accordingly. Most big brands will know how to value a package of sponsorship assets, and of course they'll choose the package with the highest ROI. In this case, it was the bronze level.

Had the rights holder priced their sponsorship levels appropriately to the value each level offered, 50 percent of the sponsors would have purchased the gold level, 30 percent silver, and only 20 percent bronze. That would have boosted total sponsorship revenue by 36 percent. A poor pricing model cost this rights holder a lot of money.

I have seen thousands of examples of overpricing and underpricing sponsorship packages, and they always cost the rights holder money. Many rights holders do this year after year. So, for example, if underpricing or overpricing costs the rights holder £50,000 each year, and the event has been going for twenty years, that organisation has lost £1 million simply because they priced their assets wrong. Over the long-term, these losses really add up. It becomes business-critical to price your assets appropriately.

Another important feature of this table is the detailed breakdown of each individual asset on offer. Rows three through sixteen list various assets, from naming rights to exhibition space to complimentary race entries, along with their corresponding value. These numbers are not estimates; they are exactly what each asset is worth. To determine the total value of the entire package, you simply add up the value of the individual assets.

The question we get asked most is, "What is my sponsorship worth?" We respond by saying, "What have you done so far to figure out what it's worth?" The answer is most often, "Nothing."

Rights holders should be able to look at a sponsorship package and value the package accurately. Brands do it. They either do it instinctively or they send it to their agency to do it. But rights holders never seem to do this.

One of the quickest and easiest first steps to determining value is called benchmarking. Just like in real estate, when an appraiser is trying to determine the value of a house, the first thing he does is look at similar houses and uncover the prices they sold for.

Music festivals are a great example. There are thousands of music festivals each year. They all sell sponsorships. So it surprises me when I meet with a music festival organiser, and they have no clue what to charge for their sponsorships, because they haven't looked at what similar festivals are charging. That would be like a realtor pricing a home for sale without looking at comps in the neighbourhood.

A music festival organiser should never say, "We need £100,000 to pay our headliner band, so let's charge a sponsor that much." That would be like listing a house for sale for £1 million because that's how much money you need to buy a sailboat, even though similar homes on the same street are selling for half that price. Just as a home will never find a buyer at double the price of what it's worth, neither will a sponsorship proposal.

Yet, remarkably, even after rights holders demand an unrealistic price for their sponsorship, they're frustrated and perplexed when there are no takers. They say, "Sponsorship is so difficult."

KNOW YOUR WORTH, BECAUSE BRANDS DO

On the brand side of this problem, there is also frustration. Brands and their marketing teams are typically more analytical than rights holders. Brands know their market. They know what similar sponsorships are selling for, so they often have a better idea of what a sponsorship is worth. When they get pitched a sponsorship that is ridiculously overpriced, they know it.

All major brands are analytical about how they spend their marketing dollars. They have formulas with which they estimate a sponsorship's potential ROI. They have the added advantage of seeing sponsorship proposals all the time. Most global brands receive more than ten thousand unsolicited sponsorship proposals in one year. That's a tremendous number of pitches.

"MOST GLOBAL BRANDS RECEIVE MORE THAN TEN THOUSAND UNSOLICITED SPONSORSHIP PROPOSALS IN ONE YEAR."

Think of it this way. If you were car shopping, you would do your research, and you'd have a pretty good idea of what the car you want to buy is worth. You wouldn't pay double what the car is worth. Similarly, neither will brands overpay for sponsorship.

However, a significant challenge arises because most of the sponsorship proposals that brands receive have no basis in research and are not priced at market value. They're priced based on the rights holder's financial *need*, not on a realistic estimate of the sponsorship's actual value. So even an astute brand management team with a comprehensive spreadsheet of past sponsorship pitches still may not have market-relevant data.

This leads to brands making poor sponsorship decisions too. Sometimes brands don't take the time to research whether a certain sponsorship opportunity is the best value, provides a reasonable return, aligns well with their customers, or delivers what they need at the moment. They just buy it. Some in the industry call this "chairman's whim."

In general, brands are better at sponsorship analysis than rights holders. I would estimate that 90 percent of rights holders don't rationally value their properties in the current marketplace, and about 50 percent of brands don't. At best, they do a rough calculation based on vague assumptions.

This is why so many sponsorship proposals go unfulfilled. Rights holders who are pitching overpriced assets have to hope that they connect with a brand that is poorly informed or hasn't done an ROI analysis. In other words, they're looking for a sucker.

YOU BET YOUR ASSETS

When I talk about "assets," it's important that you understand what that means in the branding context. In business in general, an asset is anything of value that the company owns. In sponsorship, assets are the itemised *rights* that a brand can buy from a rights holder. They could include a logo placement on something, branding on a building or inside a concert hall, exterior signage, VIP tickets, backstage passes, access to athletes, and so on. Assets should be listed very specifically and be clearly defined in the sponsorship proposal.

Assets can be confusing, because many people view sponsorship as an intangible. They see it as an idea, a concept, or an association. But it is much more concrete than that. Assets *are* the package.

I like to use a retail store as an analogy. If you go to a store, the assets are everything that's in the store. Similarly, the assets in a sponsorship rights package include everything you can touch, change, or manipulate. In a typical store, let's say there are ten aisles. Most sponsorship packages include everything in aisle one. Aisle one includes tickets, hospitality, and branding. As a store, you are so much more than aisle one.

If you owned a store and you had ten aisles, but you only sold items in aisle one, would that be smart business? Absolutely not. Because you're paying rent on a ten-aisle store. The business would not survive. Yet that is how sponsorship is set up.

The challenge is identifying what is in the other aisles. It could include your people, your skillset, your board, your front door. It's even the front of your forehead. Because if Coca-Cola offered you £50 million to tattoo their logo on your forehead, for £50 million, you'd probably do it.

Now this doesn't necessarily mean you should include all ten aisles in your sponsorship proposal, or get a face tattoo, because not everything in those aisles is valuable. You need to start thinking beyond the obvious. You have to get away from aisle one. When you start appreciating that your sponsorship opportunity adds more value to brands using other assets, then you start really understanding partnership.

Next, we have to look at how those assets are priced. Let's say two shoppers in the same store buy the exact same three items—a chicken, a potato, and a leek. But at the checkout register, one shopper pays £20, and the other shopper pays £100, for the same three things. Would you keep shopping at that store? Of course not, even if you were the person who paid £20. In effect, there's no set value of those three items, because the business is just charging whatever they want.

Another issue arises around price when it comes to what each shopper does with what they purchased. Let's say both shoppers paid the same amount, £20, for the chicken, potato, and leek. One shopper takes the chicken, potato, and leek and prepares a gourmet meal of Coq au Vin. The other shopper is a terrible cook and burns the chicken, undercooks the potato, and ends up eating a raw leek for dinner. Should the shopper who prepared the gourmet meal pay more than the shopper who can't cook? Of course not. Because they bought the exact same items. What they did with them when they got home was up to them.

And yet sponsorship people price their assets all over the place. Why? They don't know what to charge. They're not transparent. There's no consistency. They'll argue that the rights fees should be higher for brands who will make more use of them, even though the assets are the same.

If retail outlets charged in this way, we'd never shop.

SHOPPING WITHOUT A LIST?

It's surprising to me how many sponsorship proposals I see that do not list the exact and specific assets that are being offered, and fewer still have price tags. This makes no sense. You wouldn't go to Harrods and purchase a large shopping bag filled with merchandise without knowing exactly what's inside or the cost of the bag. Likewise, brands should never buy a sponsorship package without understanding exactly what it is they're buying.

SPLIT-SECOND SPONSORSHIP

The pit crew jumped into action. Literally. Their driver, the world-famous Italian playboy and Formula One legacy whose dad was a Formula One legend, was coming in hot. He was young, reckless, and arrogant. But he knew how to win. The owner didn't mind paying him £6 million per season, plus endorsements.

Disc brakes rotating at two hundred miles per hour generate extreme heat, and you could smell the smoke from the brake pads even before the car arrived. In Formula One, a complete pit stop with tyre change and refuelling can be done in as little as 2.05 seconds. That's less time than the average person takes just to grab their car keys.

In this sport, shaving a few tenths of a second is table stakes; it's expected, no big deal. The real money in this game is in cutting *hundredths* of a second. It can mean the difference between getting sprayed with Moët in the winner's circle and drinking vodka alone back in the hotel.

Formula One is famous for its prestige sponsors, such as Ferrari, Shell Oil, Foster's, and Heineken. Take one look at any Formula One track, and you'll see marquis brand names plastered all over the guard rails, the grandstands, and even the landscaping, not to mention every inch of every race car.

Formula One is built on logo-placement sponsorship. But that paradigm is beginning to change.

HIDDEN ASSETS

Most organisations have more sponsorship assets than they realise (the assets in aisles two through ten). Offering to slap a logo on something is usually the first and only asset that comes to mind. It's a good start, but that's just aisle one. Usually that's all brands and rights holders think about. Formula One only thought about aisle one for decades and made millions by selling it. By looking beyond the obvious, greater value beyond a logo could be created.

One of the interesting things about Formula One and McLaren Automotive is the amount of data and technology that's required to operate automobiles at more than two hundred miles per hour around a race course. Split seconds can mean the difference between earning millions of pounds or earning nothing. The data, computing, and engineering needed to run a successful Formula One team is astounding. Those systems and the engineers who developed them have many other potential applications. They are valuable assets, even though they're not in aisle one.

Enter GlaxoSmithKline (GSK). GSK's consumer healthcare division makes multiple different kinds of toothpaste, including the brand names Sensodyne and Aquafresh. Over the years as consumer tastes changed, GSK began producing more and more different types, flavours, sizes, and styles of toothpaste to meet market demands. The need to produce so many different types of toothpaste, and to change the lines so frequently, led to constant production problems and manufacturing bottlenecks. They couldn't change the lines over fast enough, and the existing lines didn't have the capability for real-time data monitoring and other systems. This began to cost GSK millions and millions in revenue.

Every time the manufacturing line had to switch from one type of toothpaste to another, they had to shut down the line. It was a cumbersome process. The longer the line was shut down, the more money it was costing GSK. In manufacturing, just like in auto racing, time is money. GSK's financial analysts determined that if they could reduce downtime by half, it would mean the production of an additional 6.7 million tubes of toothpaste per year. That equates to millions in additional revenue.

GSK tried to solve this problem internally with their own engineers. They couldn't do it. Then they looked outside the company to consultants, vendors, manufacturing specialists, and other experts. Nothing worked. They couldn't solve the problem, and it was costing them a fortune.

GSK began looking for new ideas and a new approach. They needed the best engineering teams in the world to solve their problem. They needed to find a team of engineers with expertise in data modelling, real-time monitoring, and management of high-volume production settings where fractions of a second are critical to success.

Someone suggested Formula One.

GSK WANTED MCLAREN'S HUMAN ASSETS

Formula One engineers are rock stars in their field. They travel all over the world. They get paid a fortune. They work in a fast-paced, high-tech production environment where every second counts. GSK decided they needed the expertise of these rock-star Formula One engineers.

There was one problem. There was no way Formula One engineers were going to give up the glamorous life of auto racing to go work at a toothpaste factory in Maidenhead, England, and GSK knew it. They realised there was no amount of money that could hire away Formula One engineers, so they had to find another way.

They reached out to McLaren Automotive, a Formula One race team. Rather than partnering with McLaren in a traditional branding deal, GSK sought a much more beneficial partnership. GSK wanted to utilise a totally different asset that McLaren had—an asset from aisles two through ten. The McLaren engineers.

GSK offered to sponsor the team, but rather than an Aquafresh logo on the car, GSK wanted the McLaren engineers in the off-season to help them sort out their production-line problem. Up until that point, Formula One had never sold their people as an asset. For decades, Formula One only sold the assets in aisle one.

McLaren agreed, and their Formula One engineers revamped the GSK high-speed toothpaste lines. Using the same data-driven engineering techniques required to compete in Formula One, McLaren was able to reduce the line switchover time by 60 percent, from thirty-nine minutes down to fifteen minutes. It was a tremendous success that made GSK millions. Years later, the McLaren line is still the top-performing line in the GSK universe.

FROM SYMBIOTIC MUTUALISM TO COEVOLUTION

Just like with some animals in the natural world, historically, brand sponsorship was built through symbiotic mutualism where two organisms of different species exist in a relationship in which each benefits individually from the other being in close proximity. For example, many people are familiar with the clownfish and the sea anemone. In this symbiotic mutualistic relationship, the clownfish protects the anemone by feeding on small invertebrates that otherwise have the potential to harm the sea anemone. In return, the clownfish is protected from predators by the stinging tentacles of the sea anemone. In this type of symbiosis, both the clownfish and the sea anemone could probably live without each other, but they choose to live together and thus reap the rewards of mutual benefit.

Similar relationships exist in the world of sponsorship. When Coca-Cola sponsored every event in the 1980s, they weren't reliant on those events to grow. They could have grown their business without those sponsorships through other forms of marketing. Sponsorship just helped them be more efficient and effective.

What is now possible with sponsorship goes beyond just symbiotic mutualism and into coevolution. The McLaren-GSK partnership exemplifies how these types of partnerships can now exist. "Coevolution" is the term used to describe cases in biology where two or more species reciprocally affect each other's evolution; they *require* each other for growth. This typically happens because of the environment and is built out of necessity.

The McLaren-GSK partnership created a closer relationship between the two companies in a way that sticking a logo on a car can't. They moved from a symbiotic mutualistic relationship where they could exist without each other, to a coevolution relationship in which they grow faster together. The teamwork between GSK and McLaren has become a long-term, mutually beneficial partnership. Together, the two companies are rolling out their proprietary high-speed manufacturing systems to factories around the world. The same technology has applications in GSK's pharmaceutical and healthcare product lines as well.

The lesson here is that McLaren Automotive had a tremendous asset in its people and systems. But they never saw it as an asset because those assets weren't in the obvious aisle. If they had realised the full nature of these assets earlier, they could have had these types of partnerships in place years before. It took a company looking in from the outside to recognise the potential of those assets.

As a result, what could have been just a standard logo-on-a-car partnership instead became something much, much bigger—it could improve manufacturing around the world. In fact, it could grow into its own multibillion-dollar business. This is an example of the value of mutually beneficial partnerships.

BUT I CAN'T VALUE SOMETHING THAT'S UNIQUE

That's an objection I often hear, and it's frustrating to no end. I hate to be the bearer of bad news, but in sponsorship *nothing is unique*. I've valued sponsorship opportunities where they shot someone into space. Not even that was unique. Let me explain.

Shooting someone into space, the activity itself, is unique. Or at least highly unusual. But all the sponsorship assets around it are not. The live broadcast of the event to the world is just another live event broadcast; it's not unique. A speaking tour by the person who was shot into space is another asset. Again, not unique. These are standard sponsorship assets that can be valued.

VALUE THE INDIVIDUAL ASSETS

It's not difficult to measure the value of sponsorship assets. When you individually itemise each one of your assets, there's a very easy, tangible way to value a sponsorship. The problem is that most sponsorship people approach it as a whole. They don't think about their assets as individual items. Quite understandably, it's difficult to value something unless you break it down into smaller parts. I'd have a hard time going to the grocery store, pulling a whole shopping bag full of items, and then estimating the price just by eyeballing the entire bag.

As an example, let's value two of the assets of the Red Bull Stratos live event that happened in 2012. Austrian skydiver Felix Baumgartner ascended thirty-nine kilometres up into the stratosphere on a helium balloon. He then jumped out of the capsule and did a ten-minute freefall in a pressurised suit, eventually parachuting safely to the ground. According to YouTube, the live webcast of the event was seen by 9.5 million people, setting a record for live views on YouTube.

The first asset to value was the total number of viewers. Based on planned marketing and PR projections from past live events on YouTube, and past daring stunts on television, it's not terribly difficult to estimate the size of the audience. Once you have that estimate, it's a simple cost-per-thousand calculation that advertisers have used for decades. Valuing the total viewership of something is straightforward.

Now let's value something a little more difficult—the speaking tour that Baumgartner did in the months after the event. To value this, we start by looking at the fees speakers get in general, and the speaker market overall. Then we look at the speaking fees that people who have been to space have received. If Baumgartner is more interesting and a better speaker than the others, we charge a little more. If he's boring, we charge less. Then we estimate the number of speaking bookings that we can secure, and so on, until we have an estimate of the total value of the speaking-engagement asset.

Prior to Felix Baumgartner, no one had ever jumped from a helium balloon thirty-nine kilometres up and safely landed back on Earth. So, in that sense, the event was unique, and some might argue it was impossible to value. But valuing the event before it happened was actually quite simple if you knew what assets to value.

BRANDS SHOULD CALCULATE THEIR EXPECTED RETURN ON INVESTMENT

Every brand that invests money into sponsorship should have an estimated or expected return on investment that they are seeking. Many sponsorships cost hundreds of thousands, if not millions. Smart brands set goals and make those expectations clear to the rights holder.

The analogy of buying groceries and cooking a meal

applies here as well. You make a grocery list because you know you're going to cook something specific. You know the intended outcome before you go shopping. The same principles apply here; brands should always think about what they're going to do with the assets before they do it, and they should know in advance what they are hoping to achieve. On the other hand, if you know you're a terrible cook, and you can't cook chicken, then you should be calling Deliveroo.

But, outside of the accounting profession, ROI means different things to different people, and brands enter sponsorship for many diverse reasons. Some brands want a sponsorship to generate actual revenue and profit by driving sales. Others want name recognition and exposure they can measure. Still others may want to pack the event with their biggest VIP clients as a thank you. Regardless of what the brand wants, there must be a tangible ROI for it to make sense.

Far too often a sponsorship value is purchased purely based on reach alone. The insurance chairman was happy to sponsor a football team just because he knew that seven million people watched the games and would see the insurance company's logo. But what value does that really provide? The trick is using sponsorship to get as many of those seven million people to do what you want them to do.

When brands spend money on sponsorship, they typically want the sponsorship to generate value all on its own. Sponsorship deals should always include an inherent ROI, at minimum through the purchase of economies of scale. Activating well then drives an even higher ROI. But if brands have to do a lot of work, then they might as well just go all-in and run their own ad campaign or create their own event.

I've encountered plenty of sponsorship deals that don't make sense because there's no inherent ROI built in. A typical example of this happens in high-profile event sponsorships. It works like this. A brand will receive a pitch for a £50,000 sponsorship package that comes with a complimentary VIP table and ten tickets. If the company's primary ROI is going to come entirely from high-level networking, they should first look at the ticket price. If you can just buy ten VIP tickets at £1,000 each, then just do that and save £40,000. I'm always surprised how often brands overpay for sponsorships when the asset they really want is a fraction of the cost of sponsorship. Just buy the asset.

START OFF THE RIGHT WAY

When sponsorship works well, it drives significant return for all parties, and most importantly, it's sustainable. The best way to make that happen is to start off the partnership in the right way. Do *not* start your sponsorship journey by saying, "We need money, and this is how much we need." Brands are not interested in how they can help you. They're interested in how you can help them.

Do yourself and your organisation a favour and start the relationship with your sponsor by saying, "This is what *we're* trying to achieve. This is what *you're* trying to achieve. Let's work together to achieve these things." It's a very different starting point, and one that will lay a solid foundation for a long-lasting relationship.

The unfortunate truth of this industry is that agencies and sponsorship professionals have learned to give lip service to that notion of mutual benefit. Everyone has been trained to say, "Let's work together toward both of our goals." In most cases, it's a lark, because they have no idea at all what it is their partner is trying to achieve.

That's part of my mission. I want to change this industry for the better. Sponsorship is currently a $60 billion industry, and it's growing every year; it shouldn't be built on conjecture, vague assumptions, crossing your fingers, and hoping for the best. This type of guesswork and volatility would not be tolerated in any other industry, and it shouldn't be tolerated in sponsorship.

REMINDER: IMPORTANT TAKEAWAYS

Succeeding at sponsorship does not happen by following just one or two of the principles in this book. It requires all of them.

CHAPTER 1 TAKEAWAY: Consumers ignore most ads. So if your marketing strategy is built only upon traditional advertising, you're wasting a lot of money for diminishing returns.

CHAPTER 2 TAKEAWAY: When trying to sell sponsorship, do not focus on yourself or your organisation. *Focus on the sponsor.* By asking the right questions, you are likely to understand their needs and thus secure the right sponsorship.

CHAPTER 3 TAKEAWAY: When pricing your sponsorship assets, don't focus on the amount of money you need. Instead, price the assets fairly, based on the actual value they provide to a sponsor.

CHAPTER 4 TAKEAWAY:

CHAPTER 5 TAKEAWAY:

CHAPTER 6 TAKEAWAY:

CHAPTER FOUR

LEARN THE FUNDAMENTALS

Planet Earth is full of incredible mysteries that boggle the mind. Stonehenge. The Bermuda Triangle. Big Foot. Loch Ness Monster. The Shroud of Turin. The Lost City of Atlantis. Extra-terrestrials.

For my money, one of the great mysteries of humanity is this: Why do organisations that rely on sponsorship revenue refuse to invest a little time and money to learn how to do sponsorship strategically? It's a mystery. Because if they did, their results would be leagues better. It's clearly not as big a mystery as Stonehenge, but it's definitely up there.

When people don't know what they're doing, they fail.

When they fail, they adopt this view that sponsorship is so difficult. It's only difficult because people refuse to invest in learning the proper way to do it.

I have seen giant brands with billions of dollars and huge rights holders with incredible assets who refuse to spend £200 to send their team to a course on how to do sponsorship better. The HRP spent a ton of money on their proposal, but they didn't invest in learning how to sell sponsorship properly. The Queen doesn't even care, and she's got unlimited resources.

One reason people don't invest in learning the fundamentals is there is a false perception that sponsorship doesn't require skill at all. A trained monkey can do it—or worse, an intern. "We'll just go knock on the doors of some brands, and they'll give us a big cheque." Then when they fail to secure a sponsor, they don't understand why. Blindly knocking on doors may have worked in the past, but it doesn't work now.

Training and education are customary in every career field. People who want to succeed in sales invest in sales training. People who work in human resources, medicine, and accounting spend hours in continuing-education classes and regular testing to keep up with best practices in their industry. But for some reason when trying to secure sponsorship revenue, most won't spend £200 to learn how to do it, even though sponsorship revenue can mean the difference in being profitable or not. No wonder so many people think sponsorship is difficult.

MAESTRO KELLY LOVELADY

The enormous dome of St. Paul's Cathedral shined brightly in the moonlight. Designed in the English Baroque style by architect Christopher Wren, St. Paul's was the perfect place for tonight's concert. The faint sound of stringed instruments being tuned filled the cavernous rotunda. When the concert began, the music spilled out onto the Festival Gardens where thousands of classical-music lovers gathered for the City of London Festival.

All eyes were on the conductor of the chamber orchestra. Even from the very back of the church, it was obvious that this maestro didn't move like a "typical" conductor—that is, a man in his fifties or sixties. Not at all. This conductor was young, vibrant, and energetic to the extreme. This maestro had long hair. This maestro was an Australian *woman* named Kelly Lovelady.

Kelly Lovelady is a gifted classical-music conductor, an exceptional artist and composer, a patron of the arts, and a wonderful addition to the London music scene. She's a female maestro in a field dominated by men. Kelly has a long list of musical accolades and accomplishments. These include joining the London Philharmonic Orchestra as assistant conductor for performances at Royal Festival Hall and joining the Konzert und Theater St. Gallen as assistant conductor for the Swiss premiere of George Benjamin's opera *Written on Skin*. She has also been singled out and presented to Her Majesty, the Queen, and His Royal Highness, the Duke of Edinburgh, as an Australian cultural ambassador. Her talent brings joy to thousands of people. Kelly lives for her passion and to share her gifts with the world. Truly inspirational.

SPONSORED BY AN ARTS PATRON

Kelly was able to live in the UK and pursue her music because of the generosity of a wealthy Australian arts patron who supported her because of her talent. Kelly lived frugally on a small houseboat in London. Any extra money she had was poured into her performances, renting music halls, paying musicians, and supporting music education.

After several years of patronage while living in the UK, Kelly ran into a problem. Her patron informed her that he could no longer support her. Kelly was devastated. Rather than give up on her dreams, she was determined to replace that income.

For a year and a half, she tried on her own to find a new sponsor, without success.

When her options had nearly run out, she came to see me and my team.

SPONSORSHIP BOOT CAMP

After meeting with Kelly and understanding her goals, I suggested that she take one of our sponsorship boot camps. This would teach her the fundamentals of securing sponsorship. But there was a problem. At the time, our boot camps cost £5,000. Kelly is an artist, not an executive; she didn't have £5,000 budgeted for such an expense. It was a big decision for her to invest a large chunk of her savings in a course to learn about sponsorship.

She had to make a difficult financial decision. Kelly saw the value in learning how to do sponsorship right, but she also had to live within her budget. She decided to pay the money and take the boot camp.

When Kelly told us she had decided to do the boot camp, I felt a lot of pressure to help her succeed, because I knew it was a huge investment for her. I knew this was a big risk and the stakes were high. I desperately needed it to pay off.

It turned out to be one of the best decisions of Kelly's professional career.

In the boot camp, we taught Kelly the fundamentals. We identified a number of things she was doing wrong. She was making the same mistakes that everyone makes: the mistakes explained throughout this book. We discarded the list of brands she had been targeting and helped her to laser-focus on a new target list. We narrowed and refined her pitch. We helped her write her sponsorship proposal. We helped her understand the fundamentals and the finer points of sponsorship.

She was ready.

After the boot camp, her results changed completely. She listened to what we said, came up with a strategy, and went out and pursued it. Within three months, she had secured three different sponsorships. Each sponsorship wasn't for a huge amount of money, but combined they were more than enough.

Getting these sponsors changed Kelly's life. Without them, Kelly would have had to move back to Australia and give up her music career in the UK. Instead, she was able to continue improving her craft, following her passion, and sharing her talents. She was so committed to her career that she was willing to spend all her money to make it happen.

A MAESTRO OF SPONSORSHIP

Of all the sponsorship success stories we've been responsible for, Kelly's story is one of my favourites. She put everything on the line and took a risk, because she believed there was a better way. And she made a smashing success of it. Five years later, she's still going strong, living on her houseboat and inspiring hundreds of thousands with her music. All this was made possible through the power of sponsorship. If Kelly was able to achieve all that with no money, imagine what a big brand or a well-funded rights holder could achieve.

This is what sponsorship education can do. Learning about sponsorship changed Kelly's life. And it helped everyone Kelly works with and the audiences she performs for. It even helped the UK music and cultural scene by helping keep her in London.

Kelly's story gives us solid takeaways. The first lesson is that finding the *right* sponsor is always preferable to finding *any* sponsor. It's even preferred over finding a huge sponsor. By the right sponsor, I mean one whose goals and values are aligned with your own. Before the boot camp, Kelly had been targeting only large organisations, when she should have been going after smaller ones that were a better match for her.

The second lesson is that Kelly succeeded because she invested in learning how to do sponsorship. She took a big risk with a lot of money. Kelly took my eight-hour sponsorship boot camp. In that one day, she was able to completely revise and hone her strategy. She was able to pinpoint a target list of potential sponsors. She was able to write a killer sponsorship proposal. She was able to understand what assets she had to offer to a potential sponsor, and how to price those assets. Once she learned these skills, they would stay with her for life.

INVEST IN BETTER OUTCOMES

In Kelly's example, a small amount of focused effort led to being able to produce a significantly different result than did the large amount of effort she had previously made. Kelly did this all by herself. She didn't have me or my team knocking on doors for her or running her campaign. She just executed what she learned.

Most people refuse to spend money on training, which means they spend years failing. A small investment could have completely changed the outcome and led to massive success.

Hundreds of organisations call us each year desperate for sponsors, but they won't invest in learning how to win sponsors properly. They're desperate, but they won't spend any money to solve the problem? The organisations that really aggravate me are the ones that want to sell their sponsorship for £500,000 and use pictures taken on their iPhones throughout the proposal. In what world does that make sense? Where else in business would an organisation say, "We're not going to invest even one pound in order to get £500,000." But in sponsorship it happens all the time. The ROI *rights holders* expect is mind-blowing. Yet they expect their *sponsors* to be delighted with a 2:1 ROI.

Kelly sticks out in my mind because to this day she is the person who risked the most to learn how to do sponsorship properly, and it worked. She listened to what we told her, and then she went out and did it. Kelly proves that anyone, even if you're a creative artist and have zero business training, can learn this stuff.

THINK OF SPONSORSHIP FIRST

Make sponsorship a strategic priority, not an afterthought. Include a sponsorship strategy in the marketing mix. Sponsorship should be a key element. Sponsorship provides value for the right partners if it's done correctly. It allows organisations to monetise something they're already doing, or monetise an asset they already own.

BIGGER IS NOT NECESSARILY BETTER

Big rights holders go after big brands, and big brands go after big rights holders. And they should. That's part of the power of sponsorship. But many organisations seeking a sponsor are much smaller. Should they still go after big sponsors?

For small- to medium-sized organisations, it's often not those big sponsors, not those big brands, and not those big rights-pullers where they will truly get a mutually beneficial partnership. Yet for some reason, every client we work with seems to want the biggest sponsor they can get. I don't mean the biggest dollar amount necessarily, although they want that too. I'm talking about the size and perceived prestige of the sponsor.

This topic comes up with clients as soon as I ask this question, "Who is your ideal sponsor?" Now keep in mind we have worked with thousands of rights holders, so we have a ton of data on this. Ninety percent of them say their ideal sponsor is the banking and financial services giant HSBC. Usually it's without putting any thought whatsoever into how *they* can help HSBC. They all want HSBC as their sponsor.

I didn't think much of this at first, but then I started to consider why rights holders all say that. There are three reasons for why everyone says they want HSBC as a sponsor. First, HSBC obviously has a lot of money. Second, they sponsor tons of stuff. Third, I believe there is a perception that having a sponsor the size of and with the prestige of HSBC will somehow cast a light of legitimacy or importance on the event or asset.

The thinking goes, "HSBC has a lot of money and they sponsor a lot of stuff. That should be the first place we go to ask for money." As it turns out, that's exactly the reason most organisations should *not* go to HSBC.

If you extrapolate that out for a minute, you can quickly conclude that every rights holder under the sun is pitching to HSBC. Just by the sheer numbers of pitches they get, the odds are against HSBC sponsoring most rights holders' events.

Furthermore, HSBC is a financial institution. They have a certain clientele that they serve. Your sponsorship may or may not align well with HSBC's needs. But your opportunity might align beautifully with a smaller financial institution, or a less prestigious sponsor.

Like many giant brands, HSBC is a huge organisation with

a massive bureaucracy. You can get lost there. Before you know it, you've spent hours and hours that turned into weeks, and still no one has called you back. Going after huge brands takes a lot of time and effort. Often that time and effort is more wisely spent elsewhere.

For these reasons, I cringe when a client names HSBC as their first choice for sponsorship. It shows the lack of thought that's gone into planning their sponsorship strategy. I'm always amazed that so many organisations put so little effort into something that is so important to them.

The same principle applies for brands. Just because a sports team has seven million fans does not mean their sponsorship package is right for you. It may be fun to brag about at parties. But that sponsorship does not necessarily mean you're getting assets that will help you deliver. Yes, the football club may have a lot of eyeballs in the stadium, but if the activation is extremely low, you've wasted your money.

It's not just eyeballs anymore that brands care about. Smaller properties will help you get a lot more leverage from their assets because they want you to be the sponsor. They want it to work, and they want to work with you. On the other hand, some of the bigger platforms, such as the Olympics, require brands to pump a lot of money and creativity into making that work. Unless you have the budget for that, a smaller platform might be better. It's not necessarily about being the biggest; it's about understanding what you have and what you can do with what you've got.

OPPORTUNITY COST OF SEEKING A SINGLE HEADLINE SPONSOR

There is a common mistake that many rights holders make, and it can cost them a fortune. That mistake is going after one big fish—in other words, a single headline sponsor. This is a high-risk sponsorship strategy and often results in devastating losses. A classic example of this is a London awards programme that we began working with in 2011.

SPONSORSHIP REVENUE TABLE

NUMBER OF SPONSORS	YEAR	APPROXIMATE SPONSORSHIP REVENUE PRE-SLINGSHOT	APPROXIMATE SPONSORSHIP REVENUE POST-SLINGSHOT
0	2000-2007	£0	
1	2007	£100,000	
0	2008	£0	
1	2009	£10,000	
9	2010	£0	
9	2011		£95,000
10	2012		£240,000
9	2013		£195,000
9	2014		£180,000
7	2015		£160,000
Total Sponsorship		£110,000	£870,000
Number of Years		11	5
Average Per Year		£10,000	£174,000
Opportunity Cost		£1,914,000	

Take a look at the table in this section. From the year 2000 all the way to 2010, this awards show ran their sponsorship efforts in-house, and their strategy was to only chase big fish. They went after a single headline sponsor and asked them to write one cheque to cover the entire sponsorship budget. As you can see, from 2000 to 2006, they failed; they didn't secure a single sponsor, so they got zero sponsorship revenue.

Then in 2007 they scored big. They secured one sponsor who wrote a cheque for £100,000. They were popping champagne corks and celebrating. There was just one problem. That sponsor didn't renew. So, the following year the awards once again went back to zero sponsorship revenue. When your entire budget relies on a single decision maker, it's simply too risky.

Once my team took over, we completely changed their sponsorship strategy and focused on securing multiple sponsors, each at a much lower price point. The awards show went from spending all their effort to chase one big fish, to catching nine or ten smaller fish. It's a better strategy to seek multiple sponsors, even at lower price points, and focus on providing value so they will renew each year. This creates a sustainable revenue model.

In the five years after we changed strategies, the awards programme raked in a total of £870,000, for an average of £174,000 per year over the five years. Now let's calculate the total opportunity cost of missing out on £174,000 per year in revenue over eleven years. That's a grand total of £1,914,000 that this award show lost because they followed a risky "one big fish" strategy. Don't do it.

You'll also notice in the table that we were able to increase the annual sponsorship revenue from £95,000 per year to more than double that. We didn't do it by dramatically increasing the number of sponsors. Instead, we worked hard to deliver value, and then we raised those sponsors up to higher levels of sponsorship the following year. One sponsor literally went from £5,000 the first year to £100,000 after they saw how much value they were receiving as a sponsor.

STOP THROWING MUD AT WALLS

Today it is easier than ever before to research brands and companies and size them up as potential sponsors. If you think a company might be a good fit for your organisation, research them online to learn everything you can about them, their values, their products, their mission, and their management team.

There are two main reasons you absolutely must do research. First, you need to narrow down your prospects to identify a list of only the ideal sponsors you want to go after. Otherwise, you're just throwing mud at a wall and seeing what sticks, which is an inefficient and ineffective approach.

You have to pinpoint the brands you think would be an ideal partner. By researching, you're doing the *opposite* of throwing mud at a wall and seeing what sticks. This principle applies to both brands and rights holders in choosing properties. Time spent doing research up-front eliminates wasting time later. This reduces the total amount of time spent looking for a sponsor.

Just as often as not, your research will reveal that a certain company you thought would be a good sponsor actually would *not* be a good fit at all. This is critically important information. It's far better to learn that early on, before you approach them. This will save everyone time and money and possibly a lot of frustration as well.

After you've prepared your target list, your research will help you demonstrate to each ideal sponsor how their values and needs align with the sponsorship you're offering. The more information you have, the better you can explain in your pitch and proposal how you'll meet that sponsor's needs.

BRANDS HAVE VALUABLE ASSETS TOO

Many brands assume all they have to offer to a rights holder is the ability to write a cheque. But their involvement in a partnership could be far greater.

In addition to cash, most brands also have mailing lists, social media followers, stores or retail locations, a warehouse infrastructure, transportation, communication channels, PR departments and contacts, talented staffs with varied skillsets, and so on. There might be a number of ways a sponsor could add value to a rights holder, other than just writing a cheque.

In many cases, brands tend to be more capable of making an impact than the event organisers themselves. Brands often have more money, greater resources, and better data, enabling them to deliver far more effective activations and campaigns.

We often suggest to our clients that they explore these options with their partners. It may be a way for the brand to negotiate a lower cash payment by offering some other important service or capability to the rights holder. You have to ask, because most brands never even think to suggest such things.

Usually both brand and rights holder have the same goal—to grow their audience. By working together, both sides gain by combining their resources and effort to create a more engaging, more impactful event, and at a lower cost to each party. This is the power of sponsorship: working collaboratively and using the synergy of resources to create something that neither side could achieve on their own.

REMINDER: IMPORTANT TAKEAWAYS

Succeeding at sponsorship does not happen by following just one or two of the principles in this book. It requires all of them.

CHAPTER 1 TAKEAWAY: Consumers ignore most ads. So if your marketing strategy is built only upon traditional advertising, you're wasting a lot of money for diminishing returns.

CHAPTER 2 TAKEAWAY: When trying to sell sponsorship, do not focus on yourself or your organisation. *Focus on the sponsor.* By asking the right questions, you are likely to understand their needs and thus secure the right sponsorship.

CHAPTER 3 TAKEAWAY: When pricing your sponsorship assets, don't focus on the amount of money you need. Instead, price the assets fairly, based on the actual value they provide to a sponsor.

CHAPTER 4 TAKEAWAY: Make sponsorship a strategic priority, not an afterthought. Include a sponsorship strategy as a key element in the marketing mix. Do your research so you can pinpoint your target list of potential sponsors. Invest in learning the fundamentals of sponsorship.

CHAPTER 5 TAKEAWAY:

CHAPTER 6 TAKEAWAY:

CHAPTER FIVE

IT'S NOT WHO YOU KNOW

Pop! Pop! Pop! The camera flashes were blinding. Behind the red velvet ropes photographers jostled each other with their giant Nikon and Canon DSLRs. The press were in a frenzy. They wanted to get the perfect shot of the talent walking down the red carpet. This was a who's who from the industry.

Cheers and squeals of delight echoed throughout the venue. The bright red carpet looked luxurious, and the step-and-repeat was covered in logos from all the top companies. One after the next, luminaries from the industry walked down the carpet, arm in arm with their dates, all decked out to the nines. They wore dresses and tuxedoes by Alexander McQueen, Stella McCartney, Burberry, Lulu Guinness, Ozwald Boateng, and Vivienne Westwood.

You could see journalists holding microphones and yelling the names of people they wanted to interview. "Brad! Brad! A question about your latest project from the *Times*?" Some of the industry luminaries would just smile politely and walk past. Others would answer a question or two. No one wanted to miss out on the fun and spectacle of the evening.

You'd be forgiven for thinking this was the Academy Awards in Hollywood. Or the Golden Globes in Beverly Hills. Or maybe the Emmy Awards or the Grammys. But if you listened closely, these people weren't talking about their new record or blockbuster film. They were talking about...cars.

And trucks. And brake pads. And shock absorbers. And tyres. Because this was not an *entertainment* industry awards programme. It was an *automobile* industry awards programme.

THE *WHAT CAR?* AWARDS

One of my very first clients was the long-running and highly successful automobile magazine and website *What Car?*

It's one of the most profitable publications of its type, and it's a top performer for parent company Haymarket Consumer Media, which owns more than fifty other titles. *What Car?* is not a magazine for automobile enthusiasts, like *Car and Driver* or *Road and Track*. Rather, *What Car?* is written for new car buyers and features an extensive buyer's guide.

For about forty years, *What Car?* has been hosting the annual *What Car?* Awards for manufacturers and automobile industry people. It's a big, prestigious event, the Oscars for car makers. They had tried to sell sponsorships but were only sporadically successful.

What Car? has one of the largest advertising sales teams in publishing. Unsurprisingly, the ad sales team was put in charge of selling sponsorships for the *What Car?* Awards. It made sense, because the salespeople already had the contacts and relationships with the companies that buy ads and would most likely sponsor the awards show. But that strategy ran into trouble.

The problem began when the title sponsor did not renew for the following year. *What Car?* was expecting that a big chunk of the budget of next year's *What Car?* Awards would be covered by the same sponsor as the year before. It was a significant financial blow when that sponsor declined.

Despite all their ad salespeople trying to sell a sponsorship, *What Car?* was having a difficult time replacing that title sponsor. They wrongly assumed that because they had a huge ad sales team and an established, prestigious event that sponsors would be easy to find. It didn't work out that way. Their sponsorship pitch just wasn't working. No one would commit. That's when they called me and my team.

I had never heard of *What Car?* before. I had no experience in publishing. I had zero knowledge of new cars and automobiles. I don't even own a car. But I explained to them in considerable detail exactly why their strategy was failing and would continue to fail.

We revamped their proposal and their pitch. Then they gave me a list of all their existing sales contacts. This was the same list that their sales team had been using successfully to sell ads in the magazine, but unsuccessfully to sell sponsorships.

We took the new sponsorship package to market. We had revised the strategy, revamped the proposal, included a specific list of assets, included exact prices, and clearly defined all the benefits and value to the sponsor. Within three months, we sold nine sponsorships for the *What Car?* Awards.

All we had was a different strategy. That's the *only* thing we changed. We didn't change anything about their event. We didn't improve or enhance the awards in any way. Their product was exactly the same. We only changed the sponsorship pitch. We presented the sponsorship opportunity in a completely different way. We revamped their pitch to focus on how sponsoring the event would benefit the *sponsor*; that one simple thing created extraordinary results.

IT'S NOT WHO YOU KNOW—REALLY, IT'S NOT

Succeeding in sponsorship isn't about whom you know. It's about figuring out what value you can offer to a sponsor and then communicating that effectively.

We used the exact same list of contacts that the *What Car?* sales team had been using. When I got the account, the *What Car?* sales team literally handed me a printed list of all their clients and their contact information. When I called that list of contacts, they didn't know me. I didn't know them. I didn't socialise in the same circles they did. Basically, I had zero relationship with those people. And I knew very little about the automobile business.

Yet we succeeded where the *What Car?* ad sales team failed, even though the *What Car?* sales reps *did* have long-standing professional and personal relationships with them.

That was another important light-bulb moment for me. It demonstrated that even though you may have friends in high places, and maybe you're already working with them in some capacity, you cannot rely on these relationships to build a successful and sustainable sponsorship programme. The *What Car?* Awards is a great event. It's very well attended by top people in the auto world, and it's put on by one of the most respected magazines in the industry. The *What Car?* ad sales team thought they could rely on the strength of the event and on knowing the right people to sell a fortune in sponsorships.

They were wrong.

Like most people who try to sell a sponsorship, they didn't realise that sponsorship requires expertise and the right approach. It requires a skillset. It requires communicating benefits and value to sponsors. The *What Car?* sales team is great at selling ads. They could potentially be great at selling sponsorships. But they didn't have the right tools in their toolkit and wouldn't know how to use them even if they did.

To add insult to injury, *What Car?* was wasting precious

sales resources by taking advertising sales executives away from selling ads to try and flog sponsorship at the awards. In addition to not getting sponsors, *What Car?* had an opportunity cost through lost ad revenue.

Having the right tools is just the start, and often the glaring lack of an effective proposal is the primary barrier to success. In proposals, effective does not just mean pretty pictures. Effective means having the right packages and being able to articulate the benefit to potential sponsors succinctly and convincingly. And, of course, ensuring the price is right.

The *What Car?* Awards is such a phenomenal event, it was shocking to learn how poor their sponsorship proposal was. Everything they thought they were doing right was wrong. They included magazine data (not awards data), the price was variable and "tailored to your level of involvement," benefits were vague, and the list goes on. Additionally, they waited too long to get their proposal in front of the right people. They also didn't plan a long-term engagement programme. The *What Car?* sales team made all the classic mistakes that cause sponsorship efforts to fail.

There are a hundred possible reasons that your sponsorship effort is failing. Please don't focus only on the things listed here. Each sponsorship and each situation is different. The joy of sponsorship is that it is varied, but it is also challenging. That's why it doesn't work to give specific how-to advice or paint-by-numbers instructions in a book. That won't help you succeed in sponsorship, because your situation will be unique. Focus instead on the important themes and ideas, and then tailor them to the specific needs of your organisation.

NOT HAVING CONTACTS IS JUST AN EXCUSE

There is a perception out there that to succeed in sponsorship you need a huge Rolodex of high-level contacts at all the major brands. I've heard people dismiss the success of others by saying, "She probably knew someone on the inside, and that's how she got that big sponsorship deal." Sorry to take away a common excuse, but that's simply not the case anymore.

When a rights holder fails to secure a sponsor, the first excuse they come up with is that they're not speaking to the right people. This is seldom the reason that no sponsor will sign on.

When organisations that are attempting to sell sponsorship come up against rejection, they mistakenly assume that it's an external problem, and they don't think they can fix it. In most cases, it's actually an internal problem.

In other words, access to the right people can't save a bad proposal. You could pitch your sponsorship proposal to the CEO in a two-hour, one-on-one lunch, but if the proposition is not right for them, you won't get a deal, and you'll be the one paying for the lunch.

THE REAL REASON NO ONE CALLS BACK

Let's say you've done a dozen sponsorship deals with the same marketing executive at a major brand. You know her. She knows you. That's a great start. But if you send over a poorly crafted proposal that fails to demonstrate value, the answer is still going to be no.

If your proposal does not clearly and quantifiably show how your sponsorship benefits a brand, there is no reason for the VP of marketing to return your call. If you're not getting to speak to the right person, it's most likely because you haven't demonstrated the value of your proposition.

If you've followed the principles I've discussed in these pages, and prepared a dynamite proposal, your odds of reaching the right person improve exponentially. When you have a solid proposal that clearly offers value to a sponsor, you don't need to be golfing buddies with the managing director. Just pick up the phone and call.

are scared of picking up the phone and calling.
, "Since I don't know anyone at that company,
get through to the decision maker. So I'm not
g to try."

Calling a stranger is scary. But when you genuinely have a good sponsorship offer that perfectly aligns with a brand, you are doing *them* a favour by bringing it to their attention. I'm not afraid to cold-call even the biggest sponsors when I have real value to offer.

A willingness to pick up the phone and call potential sponsors is essential to success. It makes no sense to spend time and resources identifying assets and preparing a killer proposal, and then stop short of calling the brands it could help the most.

My favourite cold-calling success story is one taken right out of the sponsorship industry. It outlines how success isn't just handed over—it's worked for. Former Thomas Cook boss Harriet Green is widely credited with saving the travel agent, whose shares were up tenfold just before her premature departure was announced. However, many are surprised that she was appointed by the chief executive after cold-calling the chairman and telling him, "You need me." Imagine what would have happened to the 15,500

Thomas Cook staff had she not picked up the phone. What if she thought going through a headhunter and taking the long route around would be better? Cold-calling has a very bad rap, and certainly I'm not the friendliest of people when you catch me picking up a PPI claim call. But cold-calling can also be such a great experience. It's like asking someone out on a first date. You really never know what could happen unless you take a chance and pick up the phone.

DIAL FOR DOLLARS (AND POUNDS AND EUROS)

Remember Kelly Lovelady, the music conductor? She got all her sponsors by cold-calling. She didn't know anyone at those companies. She just picked up the phone and called. As a result, she got three sponsors who changed her life.

The two important elements of that success story were a really strong proposition and persistence—also known as hustle. I think a lot of people believe sponsorship doesn't require a lot of work, as if all you have to do is write a proposal and sit back and wait for the phone to ring. That strategy doesn't work for *anything* in life, so why would it work in sponsorship? In fact, I almost titled this book *Hustle*, because that's what I attribute much of my success to: I work hard for it.

In most cases, you won't be able to connect directly with the CEO. You will have to send your proposal to a junior person and ask him or her to show it to the boss. If it's a strong proposition, and it's very clear about why the CEO or someone else high up needs to see it, it's relatively easy to get it in front of the right people. If it doesn't align, no one will want to see it no matter how many times you call.

HANDLING REJECTION

What I find unfortunate is that many people make a half-hearted effort at sponsorship, and then they give up too quickly. They make a few calls, no one calls back, and they get discouraged. Or they make mistakes, get rejected a few times, and then conclude that sponsorship doesn't work or isn't worth the time. I couldn't disagree more. There are plenty of pitfalls and common mistakes in sponsorship, but most of them are easily surmountable by changing what you think you know.

Yes, you will face your share of rejection when trying to put together sponsorships. Often it's because of reasons beyond your control. It's important to listen to the feedback you're getting from potential sponsors, and be sure to focus on the positive. If a sponsor says no to your pitch but compliments the proposal or sees the value in your assets, focus on that compliment. Use that positive feedback as inspiration to pick up the phone and make the next call. Look for positive reinforcement.

When faced with rejection, it also helps to focus on the bigger vision of what you're trying to accomplish. If you're trying to sell a sponsorship for an arts organisation, stay focused on the fact that your success will help improve the arts and culture of that community. When you think about it in this way, sponsorship becomes really inspiring. It becomes motivating. It becomes a positive experience for everyone. You have the ability to work with another partner to achieve a vision and a purpose that will benefit many other people.

Also keep in mind that rejection can lead to innovation, creativity, and growth. I've had my pitches rejected hundreds of times. People tell me no constantly. Even when the answer is no, I know we've created big ideas, built projects, and pitched really interesting things. When I get rejected, I don't take it personally. I know what my team and I are doing is right, and we're doing it the right way. Rejection is just part of the business. Instead of letting it get us down, we get creative. It's that creation, development, and innovation phase where growth happens.

LASTING PARTNERSHIPS DRIVE VALUE

One of the best things about sponsorship is witnessing

the effect that your hard work has created. The best way to drive success going forward is to form long-lasting partnerships, both for your clients and for yourself. We saw this happen with the *What Car?* Awards sponsorship.

We secured nine sponsors for the *What Car?* Awards, which was a tremendous success, but the story gets even better. The programme was so successful that the following year *What Car?* wanted to go with fewer sponsors. They said they had so many sponsors that it kind of overshadowed the award winners and the magazine itself. That's a good problem to have, especially since they had zero sponsors the year before.

Another benefit was that three of those nine sponsors had never advertised with *What Car?* before. They had such a positive experience as sponsors of the *What Car?* Awards that they signed on as regular advertisers of the magazine. This is a great example of how good sponsorships can lead to long-lasting partnerships that drive additional revenue for years to come.

Also, several sponsors in the *What Car?* Awards referred even more sponsors to us, and they became sponsors too. After that first year, the event really sold itself. The original sponsors had such a good experience and achieved such a positive ROI that they became de facto salespeople for us. They said to their business colleagues, "This event is great. You should meet with their team and get involved." You can't get a better referral than that. Success breeds success, and that is as true in sponsorship as it is in life.

That's because sponsorship done well creates a tremendous knock-on effect. The benefits are long-lasting. The only regret I have about the *What Car?* sponsorship, in my mind, is thinking about what we could have accomplished if we had started several years earlier.

REMINDER: IMPORTANT TAKEAWAYS

Succeeding at sponsorship does not happen by following just one or two of the principles in this book. It requires all of them.

CHAPTER 1 TAKEAWAY: Consumers ignore most ads. So if your marketing strategy is built only upon traditional advertising, you're wasting a lot of money for diminishing returns.

CHAPTER 2 TAKEAWAY: When trying to sell sponsorship, do not focus on yourself or your organisation. *Focus on the sponsor.* By asking the right questions, you are likely to understand their needs and thus secure the right sponsorship.

CHAPTER 3 TAKEAWAY: When pricing your sponsorship assets, don't focus on the amount of money you need. Instead, price the assets fairly, based on the actual value they provide to a sponsor.

CHAPTER 4 TAKEAWAY: Make sponsorship a strategic priority, not an afterthought. Include a sponsorship strategy as a key element in the marketing mix. Do your research so you can pinpoint your target list of potential sponsors. Invest in learning the fundamentals of sponsorship.

CHAPTER 5 TAKEAWAY: Succeeding in sponsorship isn't about whom you know. It's about figuring out what value you can offer to a sponsor and then communicating that effectively.

CHAPTER 6 TAKEAWAY:

CHAPTER SIX

—————

WHY PEOPLE AVOID SPONSORSHIP

Excuses, excuses. There are so many excuses for not succeeding in selling sponsorship. Anyone who's been around sponsorship for a while has heard them all. Sponsorship is too difficult. It's too expensive. It's too time-consuming. Sponsorship is unpredictable. It requires contacts that we don't have. It's too resource-intensive. We don't have the staff.

I've heard thousands of excuses for why sponsorship sales efforts failed. Most of them are all just rationalisations for not being strategic, specific, targeted, and intentional.

Sponsorship is no more difficult than running any other type of marketing campaign. Every marketing initiative is going to require time, money, resources, and effort.

IRRATIONAL FEAR OF SPONSORSHIP

Quite often I run into a syndrome that I call the irrational fear of sponsorship. Through my work with the *What Car?* Awards, I learned about one of their magazine advertisers, a company called Warranty Direct. This company sold automobile extended warranties, and they earned good business through their advertising in *What Car?* magazine.

I asked *What Car?* why Warranty Direct was not on my list as a prospect for the *What Car?* Awards. They said, "Forget about it. They don't do sponsorship. We've tried for years to get them to sponsor, but they're not interested. Don't waste your time."

Well, I love a challenge and a strong brand fit, so I insisted that *What Car?* put me in touch with Warranty Direct. I was determined to get them on as a sponsor. Not because I wanted their money, but because I believed it was a great strategic business move for Warranty Direct.

Unlike most automotive suppliers, which sell strictly business to business, Warranty Direct has *both* B2B *and* B2C products. They would match perfectly with the event because the *What Car?* Awards provide both B2B *and* B2C sponsorship benefits, which made it unique among other automotive events searching for sponsorship, which offered only B2B benefits. Plus, Warranty Direct already knew *What Car?* They had a relationship, and they were an advertiser.

THOSE ARE FIGHTIN' WORDS

I called and called and called and sent countless emails trying to get a meeting. I was begging, really. Finally, one day I called from an unknown phone number, and I got hold of the marketing director, David Gerrans. David is one of a kind. He's like a cuddly bear that you just want to hug. He's also a hard-nosed negotiator, which is even more effective because he does it with a disarming smile. Plus, he's known for being blunt and straight to the point. David politely, yet firmly said, "Jackie, sponsorship doesn't work."

This was a man with an impressive resume and forty years of automotive marketing experience. He told me they had no interest in meeting me because they were absolutely, positively not going to get into sponsorship. He believed sponsorship and awards shows just didn't produce marketing results.

At that time, Warranty Direct's marketing consisted of print and television ads. So, I knew they were spending money. They just refused to spend money on sponsorship.

Even though he was telling me no, it was a pleasant conversation. After hearing his very well-reasoned and logically supported explanation of why Warranty Direct would never do sponsorship, I still didn't give up. I said, "Just give me thirty minutes." I think he was surprised at my persistence, and he appreciated my conviction. He agreed to meet with me.

PITCH PERFECT

I found out I got lucky when I entered the room to find both the marketing director, David Gerrans, and the managing director sitting at the table. I had not been expecting the managing director to be there. I later learned that they both found my incredible persistence to be quite amusing and wanted to witness it firsthand.

I went in and gave them a very detailed pitch of exactly what I would do, how it would be different, and what their expected ROI would be. I even showed them a timeline. It was a very clear plan. They had never seen that before. At one point, I noticed they were smiling, and I think it was because they could tell I had way overprepared for

the meeting. They let me get through ε
thought I had won them over.

After my presentation, the managing director sa
you, Jackie, but we're not going to sponsor becausᵥ
shows don't work."

I said, "How do you know? Have you ever tried?"

They both admitted that they had not tried. That's when
I literally *promised* them that it would work for them,
because I knew it would. I explained why. I proved the
value of the proposition.

They were still hesitant. So, I ended up giving them the
sponsorship for 50 percent off, just so they would agree to
try it. I basically dragged them kicking and screaming into
a sponsorship deal. They signed a contract. I gave them
the first year for 50 percent off, but with the agreement
that if it worked as I said it would, they would renew the
following year for full price.

A GREAT PARTNERSHIP IS BORN

That first sponsorship was so successful for Warranty
Direct that they renewed for the next year. Not only did
they renew at full price, but they bumped up to the title

nsor level, which was two levels (and a small fortune) above what they had bought the previous year. It was a massive win. More importantly, it was a validation of what I had promised them in that first meeting. To date, it's been an ongoing six-year relationship, and Warranty Direct is still the title sponsor.

Sponsorship worked so well for Warranty Direct that they began sponsoring more events. They even helped *What Car?* launch a new event called the Green Awards by signing on as the title sponsor, before the event even launched. Overall, it's been a tremendous, mutually beneficial long-term relationship that helped everyone grow their business.

Warranty Direct is a great success story. Before they tried sponsorship, they firmly believed it was not for them. They thought it was too difficult, too expensive, and not worth the time and effort. Once they did it with a clear strategy, it was a massive success.

Initially, getting Warranty Direct involved took a lot of effort. I worked my ass off to get that deal. But the renewal each year since is so easy. It's not hard to sell success. A huge ROI pretty much sells itself. When the ROI is exponential, clients want to double down and spend even more. Renewal meetings are more about planning for next year than hoping to get another contract signed.

IT'S EASY TO SELL A MONEYMAKER

Another lesson from the Warranty Direct story is that valuable sponsorships tend to renew almost automatically. When the sponsorship is working and providing value, everyone wants to renew. You don't have to pitch them and sell them again each year at renewal time.

In contrast, many people in the sponsorship world are focused on short-term, quick wins, even though they know sponsorships *not* creating value have to be aggressively sold and resold every year. This is a cycle that many sponsorship deals fall into. Everyone is running around trying to get any sponsor they can, without worrying about providing lasting benefit to their partners. It's like throwing mud at the wall and hoping it will stick. When that's your strategy, you're always going to have to keep throwing mud at the wall every year. That's tough, and it's a slog.

SPONSORSHIP REQUIRES PERSISTENCE

Another important lesson from the Warranty Direct story is that it took a lot of persistence to make that deal happen the first year. I had to call and call, and I would not take "no" for an answer. I finally got in the door through sheer willpower and determination. I think they realised the only way to get rid of me was to meet with me.

Once I put in that effort for a few months on the front end, that sponsorship deal generated consistent revenue for many years afterward. This is not uncommon. Sponsorship requires persistence. That's why I always laugh in disbelief when someone says, "I emailed a few brands. They never called me back. They're not interested. They won't sponsor." Ha!

This is when the excuses come out. *We don't know the right people. Our event isn't big enough. The economy is bad. Their business is down. Our timing is off. We'll have to wait until next year.* People who make excuses tend to only see what they *can't* change, and they ignore what they *can* change.

The sad thing about excuses is they become a self-fulfilling prophecy. If you really believe you're going to fail, you will fail. It's a certainty. Because if you believe it's a waste of time, then you won't do the things you need to do in order to succeed (like picking up the damn phone and calling until you get the meeting). That will just perpetuate your belief that sponsorship doesn't work.

My favourite excuse, probably because it's flattering in a way, is this: "We can't sell sponsorship because we're not you. We can't sell it the way you and your team can sell it."

Nonsense.

I honestly believe anyone can sell it, if you know what you're selling, and you've got a solid sponsorship package. The problem is not in the selling part; it's that most people don't understand sponsorship, so they fail to put together a viable, credible package. That's why they're unable to sell.

Remember Kelly Lovelady? She's definitely *not* a salesperson; she's an artistic director. That's basically the polar opposite of a salesperson. But because she learned how to prepare a viable sponsorship package, she was able to sell it. This stuff can be learned.

I'm not special. I'm not incredibly talented at doing this stuff. I don't have magical sponsorship fairy dust. I'm successful because I know what makes good sponsorship. And maybe because I outwork everybody. But there's nothing proprietary. I don't have a special sauce. It's plain old hard work and hustle, plus wanting to create value for the people I work with. That's it. Anyone can sell sponsorship if they're willing to invest in acquiring the knowledge and skillset to do sponsorship strategically.

WHY (SOME) PEOPLE HATE SPONSORSHIP

When companies need help with legal matters, they hire a law firm. When they want to get publicity, they hire a

PR agency. That type of expertise is valued. But when it comes to sponsorship, they think, "We can do this all on our own."

For some reason, organisations are willing to roll the dice on something as important as sponsorship, which generates significant revenue. Organisations need to understand that there is an investment required to succeed in sponsorship, whether it's hiring an agency like mine or allocating internal resources.

I get frustrated and annoyed when I see rights holders make the same mistakes over and over, year after year. They seem to never learn. A typical conversation goes like this. They call us and say, "Jackie, our sponsorship is worth £150,000. Can you sell it for us?"

After I look over the assets, I say, "In the current market, and benchmarking against your competitors, your assets are only worth £70,000. It's a lot less than you thought." They never like hearing this. But it's true.

They call me a week later, and they say, "We have to raise £150,000. We have six months until our event, so we're going to hire someone else who told us they could get us £150,000." I wish them luck, but inside I'm about to scream, because I know they're going to fail.

Three months later, the phone rings. It's the same person, and she says, "We only raised £8,000, and we invested £100,000 in the event. We're going to lose money. We're panicking over here. Please help us. Can you do anything?"

I understand this is how it goes sometimes. I empathise. Then I say, "Now your event is three months away, and you're asking me to perform a miracle. I feel so badly that this happened to you. But I'm sorry, I can't help you. Six months ago, I could have gotten you £70,000 and would have worked with you to rebudget your event so you broke even. Now there's nothing I can do. Next time, please call me thirteen months in advance of your event. You need to be thinking about sponsorship that far out so we can invite future prospects to this year's event.'

RINSE AND REPEAT EVERY YEAR

Then guess what happens? Next year rolls around, and they do the *exact same thing*. I tell them what their sponsorship is actually worth. They insist it's worth way more, and they tell me they're going to sell it on their own or go with another agency who promised they could sell it for the amount they are looking for. Then they call me three months later in a panic. I tell them the same thing I said the year before.

This goes on *every year*.

In fact, I launched my sponsorship agency back in 2010, and there are still a couple of people on this hamster wheel who we started speaking to in year one and who are *still* spinning around year after year getting nowhere. We receive about ten new business calls each week, five hundred per year, and I would say 90 percent of those new business calls are from people caught in this trap. They all think their event is unique and different. They're not. Many people just never learn.

After so many calls like this, I find myself wishing people would understand that the truth they don't want to hear is better than a fabrication they do want to hear. It's human nature. I get it. If an agency is promising you exactly what you want, then that's the agency you're going to pick. Nevertheless, we always tell the truth and set realistic expectations. We are not miracle workers.

I didn't write a book to drum up business. I wrote this because I sincerely hate to see organisations with valuable rights screw up sponsorship and get burned. When that happens, everybody loses. Then more people hate sponsorship and say it doesn't work, which hurts the entire industry.

IT'S WORTH WHAT IT'S WORTH

Here's something that makes rights holders mistakenly think their rights are worth more than they really are. It's when rights holders have had a major sponsor who *overpaid* for the sponsorship in the past. Because now that rights holder is convinced that their rights are really worth that amount.

For example, a major awards show in the UK once had a sponsor who paid £850,000 each year to be the title sponsor of the event. When that sponsor decided not to renew, the awards show needed to find another title sponsor. They came to us. They were convinced it was worth at least £850,000, because that's what someone had paid for it in the past.

We work with a lot of awards events. Through benchmarking and based on their numbers and their reach, I estimated that their title sponsorship was actually worth only £300,000 to £400,000. They said, "No. We got £850,000 *last* year. So it's worth even more than £850,000 next year." They decided to hire another agency who promised them they could get £850,000.

It never happened.

They spent *three years* trying, but they didn't get a title sponsor. Had they sensibly priced their offering within the range of what the market was buying, they would have gotten a title sponsor paying £300,000 to £400,000 per year for three years. As a result, their opportunity cost was between £900,000 and £1.2 million.

It's a tough lesson to learn. The fact is just because a sponsor paid a certain amount, that does not mean that's what it's worth in the current market. That sponsor could have their own legitimate reasons for why they paid a premium. The thing that determines price is the current market.

The awards programme in question eventually did sign a title sponsor.

The title sponsor paid £325,000.

REMINDER: IMPORTANT TAKEAWAYS

Succeeding at sponsorship does not happen by following just one or two of the principles in this book. It requires all of them.

CHAPTER 1 TAKEAWAY: Consumers ignore most ads. So if your marketing strategy is built only upon traditional advertising, you're wasting a lot of money for diminishing returns.

CHAPTER 2 TAKEAWAY: When trying to sell sponsorship, do not focus on yourself or your organisation. *Focus on the sponsor.* By asking the right questions, you are likely to understand their needs and thus secure the right sponsorship.

CHAPTER 3 TAKEAWAY: When pricing your sponsorship assets, don't focus on the amount of money you need. Instead, price the assets fairly, based on the actual value they provide to a sponsor.

CHAPTER 4 TAKEAWAY: Make sponsorship a strategic priority, not an afterthought. Include a sponsorship strategy as a key element in the marketing mix. Do your research so you can pinpoint your target list of potential sponsors. Invest in learning the fundamentals of sponsorship.

CHAPTER 5 TAKEAWAY: Succeeding in sponsorship isn't about whom you know. It's about figuring out what value you can offer to a sponsor and then communicating that effectively.

CHAPTER 6 TAKEAWAY: Succeeding in sponsorship requires investment, whether it's hiring a sponsorship agency like mine or allocating internal resources. Sponsorship is not money for nothing.

CONCLUSION

THE FUTURE OF BUSINESS

The world is getting smaller. Technology enables faster communication, better data capture, and more ways to analyse information. Today we're more clearly able to understand and measure the effects of collaboration.

I strongly believe that partnerships are not only the future of marketing, but also the future of business. I believe it's how organisations will continue to grow in an increasingly competitive landscape. I know it will always remain a critically important source of funding for nonprofits and charitable organisations, especially as we see the decline in government funding.

Achieving impressive results requires a shift in mindset away from traditional ways of thinking about sponsorship. Pricing a sponsorship package based on the organisation's financial need never made any sense, and the industry will continue to move away from that model and toward pricing based on the value of assets. Change is happening across this industry, and I believe we are leading the way.

When I started my sponsorship agency, I wanted my team to do things differently. In fact, I demanded it, because I knew logo placement was becoming increasingly ineffective. Back then, no one believed me. No one bought into what I was saying. Pitch meetings were hard. We struggled. But I predicted that big brands would start pulling out of seemingly lucrative deals. Now it's finally happening.

Sponsorship should never be about getting money for nothing. People who are trying to make some quick cash will never succeed long-term. Brands who carelessly write large sponsorship cheques for no measurable benefit are acting foolishly. That's just bad business.

YOU CAN DO BETTER THAN JUST PLACING LOGOS

If your organisation or brand is still running a sponsorship programme that is based around slapping a logo on something, just know that you have so much more potential for far greater impact. I really want to encourage you to stop pouring money into logo badging. Instead, think about the broader principles you've been learning in the last six chapters, and implement them into your organisation. Shift the way you and your organisation look at sponsorship.

If you do it right, this will not only elevate your entire sponsorship programme, but it will also transform your organisation. When you actively seek out partners who are aligned with your goals, you can create mutual benefit.

A recent partnership between Rockstar Energy Drinks and a global music festival is a great example. We were representing the music festival, which had created a unique, hip, trendy, world-class event. It was a music festival set in the snow in a beautiful mountain town in the French Alps. Their goal was to sell more tickets. But the event had very low brand recognition and awareness; few people had heard of it. And they had basically no advertising budget.

That made it a challenge for us to sell sponsorships, because brands want to sponsor high-profile events. We wanted to find sponsors who could not just bring funding to the event, but could also help market the event. Rockstar Energy Drinks was perfect!

At the beginning of our first meeting, I asked the Rockstar Energy Drinks team what their goals were. They said they were looking for something interesting that they could sell into newsagents as a point-of-sale (POS) display. POS displays are the prime positions in a store, so brands usually have to pay for them. However, if the brand has something cool that will attract customers into the store, then they don't have to pay for the POS.

Rockstar Energy Drinks was looking for something hip and cool that would allow them to get prime positioning in retail stores without having to pay. It was especially important because Rockstar Energy Drinks was launching a new product, and they wanted to launch it with POS displays. It just so happened that their new product had to be served cold, and they were looking for a suitable partner.

When we met, I knew this partnership was exactly what the music festival needed. It needed marketing. It needed brand exposure. The objectives of Rockstar Energy Drinks and the winter music festival were fully aligned. It seemed like a great fit on many levels. So we partnered with Rockstar Energy Drinks to run a contest. The winners would get an all-expenses-paid trip to the music festival and a ton of free Rockstar Energy Drinks.

It was a mutually beneficial partnership that lifted up both organisations. It worked so well because both understood the other's objectives. Rockstar Energy Drinks helped the music festival almost as much as the festival helped them. Rockstar Energy Drinks promoted the contest in POS displays and on their packaging, which drove ticket sales and awareness. In return, the ticket giveaway helped Rockstar Energy Drinks get free POS placements in hundreds of stores. Both partners got something extremely valuable that they probably couldn't have done on their own.

SEEK TO UNDERSTAND YOUR PARTNERS

Many of the strategies in this book are based on asking questions to uncover what it is that each partner wants. It took some research and lots of questions for Rockstar Energy Drinks and the music festival to understand what the other was hoping to accomplish. Once that information was revealed, it became clear that their interests were aligned. When partners have aligned interests, great things can happen.

This is common sense, right? It sounds obvious, because it is obvious. But I can tell you that this type of dialogue rarely happens. Sponsorship conversations usually revolve only around money. They sometimes turn into purely financial negotiations instead of both partners looking at the bigger picture.

For example, when a brand is negotiating with a major sports team, neither side typically asks the question, "What are you really trying to accomplish?" The brand rarely asks what the sports team's long-term goals and objectives are. But they absolutely *should* ask this question.

Is the team trying to build a new stadium? Grow their audience in the Middle East? Appeal to women? Start an after-school sports programme? Or establish a charitable foundation in Africa? Wouldn't those all be important things for a brand to know? Maybe that brand could provide assistance that would prove to be far more valuable than just writing a cheque.

Whether you're a brand or a rights holder, you have to understand your potential partners. If you're going to truly collaborate with someone, but you don't know where they're going, how will you help them get there? How are your efforts going to be mutually beneficial? We are adamant about asking these types of questions and fully understanding the objectives of our clients and partners. Without this information, achieving a long-term, mutually beneficial partnership is going to be difficult.

PUT PARTNERS FIRST

After so many years of focusing on just sponsorship, we

have seen it all. We understand what it takes to make good sponsorships that turn into long-term partnerships. There's nothing magical about what we do. Now that you've read this book, you know most of what we know, even though you haven't practised it as much. If you put it into action, you will be ready for sponsorship success.

I know I've given you a lot of information to think about. You probably won't remember it all. That's okay. You can always refer to some of the key chapters at any time, or review the appendix at the back of the book.

If there is just one concept or principle that I want you to walk away with, it's three simple words: put partners first. Just remember to always think about how you're going to make sure your *partner* succeeds, not just how *you* are going to succeed. If you do that, then your sponsorship will succeed. It's really that simple.

MY WISH FOR YOU

I know this book won't set the world on fire, and it's unlikely to revolutionise the sponsorship industry, but I think it's a push in the right direction. After reading these pages, I hope you'll re-evaluate your mindset and start to make changes in your approach. Maybe that means educating yourself on the latest trends shaping this industry or finding a way to glean the experience you need. Maybe it means recognising for the first time that sponsorship should be a pivotal part of your business strategy.

Sponsorship doesn't have to be difficult, but if you don't do it strategically and with a pinpoint focus, it will seem that way. Two heads really are better than one, and when you put your head together with a true collaborative partner, the results can be extraordinary.

AFTERWORD: THE STORY OF SLINGSHOT

BUILDING A GLOBAL SPONSORSHIP AGENCY

I'm not a sponsorship goddess. Far from it. I don't even consider myself a sponsorship guru. I have no special God-given talent or genetic gift that allows me to secure sponsorships where others couldn't. Everything I know about sponsorship I learned through trial and error, and by failing. A lot.

My career in sponsorship began with many years of swimming upstream against a strong current. I can't tell you how many times I was told no. For starters, I am a woman, and I work in an industry that is dominated by male sports. Seventy-one percent of all sponsorship spending is on sports. But I'm *not* a sports fan. I don't need to be. I believe professionals in the sponsorship world do not need to be passionate hobbyists, fanboys, fangirls, or alumni of the organisations they're working for. This applies to sports teams, the Olympics, arts organisations, music festivals, tourism and events, and many other types of organisations.

Yet, for some reason, there has always been a bias in favour of hiring former football players to work in football sponsorship. Or there's the belief that you should hire former Olympic athletes to work in Olympic sponsorship. It's as if being able to run fast or kick a ball somehow means you know sponsorship better. The notion that in order to sell rugby sponsorships you must be a passionate rugby fan is silly. On the contrary, I believe it's one of the reasons for the failings in the sponsorship industry today and its lack of growth. If the London Ballet wants to sell sponsorships, probably the *last* person they should hire is a former ballerina.

Like any other industry in the world, they should be hiring an experienced sponsorship professional who is passionate about forging effective partnerships and building value for all the stakeholders in a sponsorship deal. *That's what I'm passionate about.* That's what I've spent the last decade learning to accomplish in the best way possible.

Further, I believe that when you're not a passionate fanboy of something, you actually have better judgment, because you're impartial. You can see the true value of assets, unencumbered by personal desires, passions, or blind loyalty. It has been my experience that an outsider can offer a valuable perspective that someone who grew up in a certain organisation or industry cannot. An experienced sponsorship professional will always be more likely to succeed than, say, a former rugby player who is now just learning the skill of sponsorship and starting from square one.

HUMBLE BEGINNINGS

I fell into the sponsorship industry by accident. I grew up in Canada, then moved to London in my early twenties. My first job was with the Direct Marketing Association (DMA). I worked for them as a freelancer first, and then they offered me a job in sponsorships. I said, "I'll take the job if it comes with a work visa." They agreed, and I've been in London ever since.

At the time, I knew little about sponsorship. I had a vague

notion of what it was, but I had no real experience. I was forced to learn it from scratch, motivated by the desire to keep my job and my work visa. I tried to learn everything I could about the sponsorship industry as a whole and about selling sponsorships. I read books, blogs, and case studies. I asked industry insiders for tips and advice, and I spent many late nights at the office.

My commitment to learning and my determination to succeed paid off. In my first year, the DMA set a goal for me to bring in £50,000 in sponsorship money. I brought in £187,000.

By my third year, I was bringing in half a million pounds. I learned a lot in those early years of getting my feet wet in sponsorship; but truth be told, I was mostly just petrified of getting fired and losing my visa. So, I worked hard and felt lucky to have a job.

When I was twenty-four years old, after a couple of years on the job, I went to the CEO and told him I wanted to apply for a promotion, to a commercial director position with the DMA. The CEO said no. He told me I was too young and inexperienced. I accepted the feedback. I decided to keep working hard, and I got my master's degree in finance. It was a setback, and it hurt to get passed over for such a great opportunity in which I knew I could excel. Everyone who has ever been passed over for a job or a promotion knows how much it stings.

Then to make matters worse, the CEO hired someone for the role of commercial director who was incompetent, not to mention a total jerk. He was one of those people who would steal your ideas and then pass the idea off as his own. Yet he was my new boss. I couldn't stand working for him. I knew I had to leave.

Without family in the UK, I had no safety net. I also couldn't apply openly for jobs, because I didn't want to lose the one I had, and therefore my visa.

Nevertheless, I quietly approached every sponsorship agency I could. I thought that working in sponsorship would be a good match for my skillset and experience. What I hadn't realised was that sponsorship agencies dealt mainly in sports. Working at the DMA, I hadn't done anything sports-related, and the agencies I spoke to didn't see my experience as transferable. I thought that made no sense.

I applied to more than a dozen different agencies, and not one would sit down and meet with me. It was a demoralising experience. The only organisations willing to give me a shot were other trade bodies, because I had worked for a trade body. They saw value in my experience, and I even got a couple of job offers. But having already worked for a few years at a trade body, I wanted to do something different.

THE RENT IS DUE

As the rejections piled up and no agency job offers materialised, things were getting steadily worse with my boss, the commercial director. One day, I decided I'd had enough. I snapped. I looked him straight in the eye and told him I just couldn't work for him anymore. I was done.

I found myself out of a job with just £2,000 pounds in the bank. But I had my apartment, I could pay rent for a couple of months, and I had my laptop. I figured I could pay the rest of my bills by doing freelance work until the right job came along. I was twenty-six years old.

The first thing I did was start calling those trade organisations that had offered to hire me full-time. I didn't ask them for a full-time job. Instead, I began offering my services on a part-time or contract basis. And guess what? It worked. They agreed. I was officially a "consultant." I even came up with a cool name for my little company—Slingshot. I was excited to be working for myself for the first time ever.

I was my own boss, but I assure you, my self-image at the time was *not* grandiose. In fact, it was the opposite. I didn't think of myself as a CEO. (I still don't.) I wasn't a visionary entrepreneur out to change the world, like Elon Musk with SpaceX or Tesla. I started my company humbly and out of sheer necessity. It wasn't that I wanted to be rich, but because I needed to pay the rent. I had no choice but to succeed.

A GAP IN THE MARKET

As I was working freelance, I began attending conferences and seminars in the sponsorship world, looking for more clients. After working at the DMA and reading books and agency blogs for a few years, I had gained a solid knowledge of sponsorship. I still had a lot to learn, and I was far from being considered a pro.

Yet the things I saw at those conferences surprised me.

I was shocked to see how the major sponsorship agencies in London were lagging behind in basic marketing tools and practices. For example, one speaker did a presentation about the most basic level of using Twitter. He literally walked the audience through what a Twitter handle is and how to set up their first Twitter account. In contrast, at the DMA, we were using some fairly advanced Twitter analytics, and I had helped major global brands launch sophisticated Twitter campaigns and social media profiles.

At the DMA, we were selling sponsorships for a modest £10,000 to £187,000. Yet the DMA ran more robust and sophisticated campaigns than organisations with budgets well into the *millions* of pounds. This level of disparity blew my mind. I realised that at that time few big agencies were thinking and executing strategic, analytical, data-driven sponsorship programmes. They were approaching sponsorship in the same old way that they'd been doing it for decades.

These big, established agencies were asleep at the wheel. There was a need in the marketplace for a modern, analytical, data-driven, forward-thinking sponsorship agency that would use cutting-edge tools and social strategies to achieve better results for both rights holders and brands.

I was also a bit miffed that none of the premiere agencies thought I was worthy of hiring. Yet they were still doing it old-school. That's when I began blogging, commenting, and guest-posting about my thoughts on the topic of sponsorship and mutually beneficial partnerships.

During this period of my life, I had plenty of free time. I had little money and could barely make rent, so I wasn't going out or socialising much. I was just happy to have a roof over my head.

Soon, my content was getting picked up by the broader media outlets. One of the largest sponsorship magazines published a feature story about one of my articles. It ended up getting the attention of the largest sponsorship conference in the UK.

I wrote a comment about gaming on an online magazine article, and a lot of people read it. That earned me an invitation to speak at one of the largest gaming conferences. Soon, I started doing more speaking about sponsorship, and my talks resonated with people. At that time, I had different views on sponsorship than most people did. No one had been talking about sponsorship the way I was.

Meanwhile, the amount of work I was getting as a freelancer snowballed. Soon, through a friend of a friend, I was hired to do work for my first celebrity client, the American recording artist Prince. After that, I consulted with the Rolling Stones, major global brands, and other big-name clients.

At that time, I viewed freelance contract work as nothing more than a stopgap measure to generate some income while I was "between jobs." Little did I know that Slingshot would grow to become a global sponsorship agency with marquis clients around the world.

Through sheer hustle and hard work, I learned a lot about sponsorship. I'm not a genius. I can't stress this enough; everything I've done, you can do too. Armed with this knowledge and perspective, you can achieve and exceed the level of success I've had in sponsorship. My goal is to get you there faster.

WHAT SLINGSHOT DOES

Gradually, I pitched to and won more and more new clients. Slingshot slowly grew from a steady freelance income into an actual real company. Soon after, I had employees, an office, and loyal clients.

Today, our primary business is helping rights holders get sponsors, and we do this in a number of ways. We hold sponsorship training days, and we conduct sponsorship boot camps. Our primary business model is we essentially become the commercial department for a rights holder. We become their sponsorship manager. We sell sponsorships for them and handle the entire process from start to finish.

We do all of the strategic insight. We generate all the leads.

We identify the assets. We take it to market and sell it. We write and execute the contracts. Then we account-manage the process all the way through to overseeing the event and then tracking the data and metrics after the event.

That's how Slingshot has a 360-degree view of the sponsorship industry. We know the market and every facet of sponsorship. We don't just sit on the activation side. We don't just sit on the sales side.

We specialise in great sponsorships that focus on forging meaningful, mutually beneficial partnerships between brands and rights holders. Our sponsors love our rights holders, and our rights holders love our sponsors. We create value for all the parties involved. Everyone loves the process and is thrilled with the end result.

Another unique element of Slingshot is that we don't focus on sports sponsorship, which is the biggest revenue generator in sponsorship. That means we had to become more innovative and expand into a full-service, 360-degree sponsorship agency. Other sponsorship agencies that handle sports typically approach all their clients from the mindset of sports sponsorship, but that doesn't work outside of sports. In fact, it's even beginning to fail *within* sports. Having to be innovative in a smaller market, but still landing big sponsors and driving them away from sports, is what gives us such unique insights. Those insights are the basis of this book.

WE TELL CLIENTS THE TRUTH

In the sponsorship world, most agencies are anxious not to upset potential or existing clients. They tell the client what the client wants to hear, even if it means doing the same thing as last year but promising different results. That's Einstein's definition of insanity. We don't do that.

Our philosophy is, "Always tell clients the truth," which is a rare commodity. We do this even if it means losing business to another agency. Giving an honest opinion sometimes means telling even the largest clients that their expectations are unrealistic. We would rather lose the client than promise something we know we can't deliver.

In fact, quite often when we meet with a client for the first time, we say, "What you are going to hear from us is different from what all the other agencies are going to tell you. We approach things differently."

APPENDIX

THE SIX KEY TAKEAWAYS

Succeeding at sponsorship does not happen by following just one or two of the principles in this book. It requires all of them. Refer to this page often to refresh your memory and to make sure you understand and utilise all six key principles.

CHAPTER 1 TAKEAWAY: Consumers ignore most ads. So if your marketing strategy is built only upon traditional advertising, you're wasting a lot of money for diminishing returns.

CHAPTER 2 TAKEAWAY: When trying to sell sponsorship, do not focus on yourself or your organisation.

Focus on the sponsor. By asking the right questions, you are likely to understand their needs and thus secure the right sponsorship.

CHAPTER 3 TAKEAWAY: When pricing your sponsorship assets, don't focus on the amount of money you need. Instead, price the assets fairly, based on the actual value they provide to a sponsor.

CHAPTER 4 TAKEAWAY: Make sponsorship a strategic priority, not an afterthought. Include a sponsorship strategy as a key element in the marketing mix. Do your research so you can pinpoint your target list of potential sponsors. Invest in learning the fundamentals of sponsorship.

CHAPTER 5 TAKEAWAY: Succeeding in sponsorship isn't about whom you know. It's about figuring out what value you can offer to a sponsor and then communicating that effectively.

CHAPTER 6 TAKEAWAY: Succeeding in sponsorship requires investment, whether it's hiring a sponsorship agency like mine or allocating internal resources. Sponsorship is not money for nothing.

CONTACT JACKIE

JACKIE FAST is recognised as a trailblazer within the sponsorship and wider business community—specifically helping the world's leading brands, celebrities, and rights holders capitalise their revenues through sustainable sponsorship. She speaks regularly on the topics of entrepreneurship, shifting consumer trends, influencer marketing, sponsorship sales and activation, and diversity in business. Enthusiastic as much as controversial, her keynotes resonate with her audience, and her approach is a change from the usual speaking circuit.

To contact Jackie, please visit JackieFast.com.

To learn more about sponsorship, please visit SlingshotSponsorship.com.

Made in the USA
San Bernardino, CA
15 March 2018